# Praise for
## *The Performance Power Grid*

"*The Performance Power Grid* gets it right. Improving corporate effectiveness depends greatly upon determining the fundamentals that solve the performance puzzle. Giannetto and Zecca articulate important fundamentals that organizations must get right to excel. Namely, senior management garners power to change the dynamics when they achieve true clarity of their situation and the need for every individual in the enterprise to understand how the mission relates specifically to their role."

—Stephen C. Savage, SVP Integration/Planning,
Computer Associates

"As a senior financial executive in a large public company, I am always looking for ways to improve our performance. *The Performance Power Grid* is a must read for any financial executive looking for a performance methodology and keen insight into the varied issues financial executives face on a day-to-day basis."

—Karen Maloney, CFO, Scholastic

"I long believed that there was a better way to provide my organization with the information it needed but there were always too many moving pieces and too much scattered information. Giannetto and Zecca brought a clarity and focus to our environment that set us on the road to greater performance. *The Performance Power Grid* captured that process and puts it in terms that can be applied to any organization wishing to achieve and sustain greater performance. Not only a must-read, but a must-do."

—Lawrence Yellin, Controller, FujiFilm USA

"David Giannetto and Anthony Zecca frame the essential elements of organizational excellence, and through their grid they've created a compelling, programmatic approach for success. *The Performance Power Grid* is a practical, insightful, hands-on blueprint for optimal business performance."

—David Blansfield, Publisher, *Business Performance Management* Magazine

"Everyone is talking about [business] performance management. While there are lots of books filled with esoteric theories about how to increase performance in an organization, *The Performance Power Grid* presents a simple but compelling proposition: If you want to improve performance, make sure that you get everyone on the same page, align the organization from boardroom to cubicle, and your performance will improve. Practical advice that everyone should heed."

—Jonathan D. Becher, President and CEO, Pilot Software

*"The Performance Power Grid* makes business performance management practical and easy to adopt. It provides the direct examples necessary for socializing and improving performance in any business."

—Mark Smith, CEO and EVP Research, Ventana Research

"I highly recommend *The Performance Power Grid*. With it, CEOs finally have a proven methodology at their disposal that will create and sustain superior organizational performance."

—Dieter Weissenrieder, CEO and Owner, Weiss-Aug

"If you want your organization to focus on the true measures of success, *The Performance Power Grid* is required reading."

—Larry Schaefer, VP and CFO, Myron

# The
# Performance
# Power Grid

# The Performance Power Grid

## The Proven Method to Create and Sustain Superior Organizational Performance

**DAVID F. GIANNETTO**
**ANTHONY ZECCA**

John Wiley & Sons, Inc.

Published by John Wiley & Sons, Inc., Hoboken, New Jersey.
Published simultaneously in Canada.

For general information on our other products and services please contact our Customer Care Department within the United States at (800) 762-2974, outside the United States at (317) 572-3993 or fax (317) 572-4002.

Wiley also publishes its books in a variety of electronic formats. Some content that appears in print may not be available in electronic books. For more information about Wiley products, visit our web site at www.wiley.com.

*Library of Congress Cataloging-in-Publication Data:*

Giannetto, David F., 1968–
    The performance power grid : the proven method to create and sustain organizational performance / David F. Giannetto, Anthony Zecca.
       p.   cm.
    ISBN-13: 978-0-470-05144-3 (cloth)
    ISBN-10: 0-470-05144-2 (cloth)
    1. Organizational effectiveness.   I. Zecca, Anthony, 1946–   II. Title.
    HD58.9.G5   2006
    658.4'01—dc22

                                                                    2006015622

Printed in the United States of America.

10   9   8   7   6   5   4   3   2   1

# Contents

# Contents

# Author's Note

How did we get here? How did we accumulate all the problems of the modern-day business environments we work in? At what point did villagers stop laboring together, toward common goals in their villages and the fields that surrounded them, and enter the modern-day silos that we all typically find ourselves in? It happened much further in our past than most people would believe.

In the early 1600s, England allowed the ruling class, barons who controlled vast estates of property, to simply take the land of nearby peasants who looked to these barons for protection. The haves quite literally took everything from the have-nots. The have-nots (who then quite literally had nothing, no land to work, no ability to feed their families), were left with nothing to offer in exchange for the things they required to stay alive, except the sweat of their labors.

This hostile takeover forced the peasants to reduce their labor into daily-sized parcels, which they could then sell back to the barons for money (a fairly new concept at that time). These barons would later earn the very literal title of *robber-barons*. This fundamental change caused the peasants, the laborers, to commoditize themselves; they were trading their lives in order to live—their effort for food. They did not willingly trade away their uniqueness; it was taken from them forcibly. There was no need for uniqueness in the new wage-labor economic model.

These events shifted a worker's focus away from the *quality* of their work onto the *quantity* of work they could perform. The more they produced, the more they earned. From their perspective it made no sense to produce anything above the minimum accepted quality because it only detracted from the total quantity of work they could perform. Quantity was all that mattered; quantity put food on their table; quantity was all they were judged upon (except for a select few, the most sought-after artist types). That forced mental shift within the workforce at large underlies the very foundation of our modern business environment. From that moment on, it was all downhill; the modern-day economic model had just been created and workers entered the modern business environment.

Today the effects of this commoditization are so deeply ingrained that it is difficult to even conceive their impact. An organization, when viewed as a living, freestanding entity, is not reliant upon any of us as individual parts. We can all be replaced; our uniqueness is not critical to success (if it is, the organization is accepting a level of risk that is not in its best interest). This is not to say that our individual abilities do not affect the degree of success (or failure) that the organization will achieve, simply that the basic, underlying premise of employment today is based upon individual dispensability. This affects an hourly, unionized worker just as much as it does a millionaire CEO.

This background is presented to put the Performance Power Grid methodology in its proper perspective. It is working to undo 400 years of bad learning; it is working against an economic model that undermines the very things businesses need most to succeed, and to sustain success. To achieve these things, a new perspective and a new approach is required.

Throughout this book you will read that the Performance Power Grid is a *practical* methodology. To be effective, it must be applicable by today's management in any of the diverse environments in which they work; it must affect change; it must take the organization beyond the simple implementation of a new initiative to the actual realization of improved performance—those are the standards of its success. Therefore, to be practical, this book focuses on the problems of today and provides the solution that will allow these problems to be overcome. It does not focus on 400 years of history and broad economic models. However, it is important to note that each component of the methodology itself, and each step in the process that puts it in place within an organization, was built to take these broader issues and the problems they have created into account, compensating for them and the effect they have upon the people that still remain laboring.

—D. Giannetto

Learn more about *The Performance Power Grid* at
http://www.performancepowergrid.com.

# Preface

You're a busy executive or manager with a lot on your mind, days full of challenges, balancing work with family life. Why take the time to read another book about how to improve your company? Because, quite frankly, this book will make your life on and off the job a lot easier.

*The Performance Power Grid* describes a highly effective, yet profoundly simple approach to managing. It is an approach that can permanently improve your organization's performance without trying to change you, your organization, or anyone in it.

We have done it with organizations and seen it work. Together we have over 45 years of experience in business. For over 30 of those years we have worked with companies specifically to improve their performance. We both have held high-level management positions in large companies where we were charged with improving performance. We have experienced, and continue to experience within our own organization, the same issues that managers face each day.

We have worked as consultants for start-up companies, middle-market companies, and some of the largest multinational and not-for-profit organizations in the world. All shared common problems. They could not achieve and sustain superior performance. Sometimes they rose to the top of their industry but failed to remain there. They could not overcome age-old organizational issues.

For those organizations we worked with, the Performance Power Grid corrected all that. It built a management framework that allowed them to evolve beyond their current environment and its culture, beyond the constant obsession with what went wrong. It moved companies past traditional budgeting, forecasting, and reporting solutions. It focused attention on *revenue, profit,* and *customer value*—the true measures of success in business.

Our award-winning management framework improved organizational performance because it took into account how employees naturally act and interact; it didn't try to change them. Its success sprang from its ability to create an environment where each person evolved naturally toward superior performance and organizational success.

Our approach is *not* traditional. Traditional management models frustrate employees. These models expect people to understand high-level objectives without clearly articulating how those objectives pertain to them. Traditional models also demand greater dedication and devotion to the organization, yet they fail to provide employees with the tools and information they need to make them more successful and their jobs easier.

Only by bringing people together around the things that matter most to a company can organization-wide superior performance be achieved and sustained. The Performance Power Grid doesn't talk about building teams; it builds them. It doesn't encourage employees to leave the protection of their individual silos; it draws them out naturally. It doesn't waste time telling people to change; it simply focuses them on those things that truly drive the success of the organization. Employees willingly embrace the power grid because it makes their jobs easier and more fulfilling.

# Preface

Without any big fanfare, the power grid dramatically improves revenue, profit, and customer value.

The Performance Power Grid works even when co-workers are not friends or find themselves at odds. Players on a team and soldiers in combat often do not like one another or have little in common, yet they work in unison toward a common goal. We bring those dynamics to the corporate world.

Imagine the power of unifying the actions and efforts of every employee within your organization, from the boardroom to the cubicle, from the accounting and finance out to the edge of the enterprise. Imagine them focusing their time and effort on the things that truly drive the success of the organization despite constant distractions. Imagine the increase in effectiveness and efficiency when they have easy access to the information they need—*right now*. Imagine that they can see and understand the future, not just the past. The Performance Power Grid drives organizational performance and success to the level that management has always known possible but has been unable to achieve.

This methodology was created to meet business needs, and uses today's best technology as an enabler. Using this technology it translates strategic objectives into actionable, measurable information. It then places that information at the fingertips of decision makers at every level of the organization. The grid shows executives, managers, and knowledge workers (those employees who are not management but still require specific information with which to make better decisions) where they stand today—right now. It focuses their effort away from the noise and fires common to most environments, and onto the organizational issues that are truly important. It then answers employees' most frequently voiced question: *Why?* "Why is this important to me? Why are we failing?" Or even, "Why are we succeeding?"

Traditional management reporting models only give employees half the picture. A scorecard tells them what their performance was, but it does not tell them what actually caused it. Before they can take real action or even make an informed decision, they must then get up from behind their desks and go find out, from another source, *why*. Only by understanding both what performance is, and why it is what it is, can management then take immediate action. Managers are often forced to circumvent this process by simply making the best decision they can based upon what they know, or what they intrinsically believe, about their organization. Therefore, the results often don't achieve the desired end. In addition, people will often make the extra effort or go the extra mile if they understand why something is critical to their personal success. Logic then says that it is the organization's responsibility, and in its own best interest, to ensure that its best interests and its employees' are one and the same.

To bring this all together, the Performance Power Grid functions like an electrical power grid. Each day we expect electricity to be there for us. We consider it something constant in our lives, something always available. Such a grid shapes the very fabric of our lives and influences nearly everything we do. However, behind the scenes an electrical power grid isn't constant at all. Out of sight it is drawing power from the sections of the city that don't need it and applying it to those that do. It is helping everyone live better, easier, more fulfilling lives. An electrical power grid is actually in a state of constant flux and change. It is a limited resource; it can run out.

So too is power within our organizations. Time, money, and human energy are all limited resources; they can run out. How does an organization use this limited power to make itself better and everyone's job easier? The answer: There needs to be an organization-wide power grid behind the scenes, moving and focusing power where it is most needed.

Your challenge is also simple. Are you willing to open yourself to a new management approach? Are you willing to accept and move beyond the way employees within an organization currently act and interact? If so, let's get started.

# CHAPTER 1

# The Performance Puzzle

**...**

In early July 1863, the United States had been engaged in a great civil war for over two years. That summer Confederate General Robert E. Lee led his undefeated army north into southern Pennsylvania where he hoped to inflict a great defeat on the Union Army. For three momentous days the two armies locked in battle at the small town of Gettysburg. It proved the turning point of the war.

As the battle raged, Brigadier General G. K. Warren, Chief Topographical Engineer of the Union Army, climbed to the top of Little Round Top, a largely barren hill standing just beyond the farthest point of the Union left flank. The site, which held a commanding view of the entire battlefield, was being held by a small group of Union signalmen. From this location they could see troop movements and reliably estimate their numbers, check on the placement of key artillery, and relay this critical information to the field commanders.

To perform this task Warren had withdrawn from the center of the battle, where his units were currently engaged in a fierce battle. His own brigade had lost a number of men that day, and it was likely more would fall, but by and large his men knew what to do, and the signalmen required checking. Warren understood that without the insight of the signalmen the Union generals would be largely blind, unable to move artillery as needed, and they would not know what key terrain now held a threat or what areas on the front lines required strengthening. These were his army's keys to success.

With this in mind Warren went to Little Round Top and from there could see for himself the Union Army stretched below in the shape of a fishhook. His new vantage over the battlefield gave him fresh insight into how the battle would unfold. The entire line lay exposed to his view and his concern was immediate. He could see that Little Round Top was a key position that could spell failure if lost, yet a pitiful handful of signalmen were holding it. Disturbingly, from his new perspective, he could see Confederate forces advancing on the position.

The consequence of losing Little Round Top was obvious to him. As an engineer he knew that if the Confederates seized the hill they would quickly place their artillery on it and the entire Union line would be subjected to a constant, deadly barrage of cannon fire. Under this fire, the line would certainly break and the battle would be lost. Almost unbelievably, the most important position on the battlefield was being held by the most meager of forces.

Warren ordered the signalmen to relay a request for immediate troops, and in short order a portion of his own brigade arrived to provide the initial defense of the position. A token force of artillery under the command of Lieutenant Charles Hazlett also responded. Although the prospects for his survival were slim, he understood the value of his position and threw his forces into action. He was killed later that day defending Little Round Top.

Had Warren not seen the vulnerability of the Union lines to enemy artillery firing from this position and taken quick action, the Confederates would likely have won the Battle of Gettysburg. Washington D.C. would have been taken or, at the least, besieged, and the course of the war would have been altered, perhaps permanently. As it was, the battle continued throughout that day and the next, and in the end the Confederate forces withdrew and returned to Virginia. The war was all but over, though tens of thousands were yet to die.

■ ■ ■

Perspective matters. If General Warren had not disengaged himself from the chaos of the front line, pulled himself off the battle line, and made the extra effort to climb Little Round Top, he never would have observed the panorama of the battle. From his bird's eye view he could clearly discern the Union's strategic needs. Had a different soldier been in his position, one not armed with Warren's personal knowledge of artillery and battle formations, he may not have noticed his army's vulnerability.

Why hadn't the men already on Little Round Top alerted their army of its danger? Possibly, they were too caught up in their own tasks and failed to consider the consequences of what was taking place just below them. Looking out for the entire Union Army was not typically the responsibility of a signalman.

Today's senior managers may not have to risk life and limb defending hilltops, but they do fight their own important battles every day. The keys to their success are surprisingly similar to what General Warren did at Gettysburg—clearly understand the objectives and then focus unwavering attention upon each action that contributes to their achievement. Clear objectives are a white line on the otherwise confusing field of battle that says, "This is the goal line—this is where we are heading—getting here is success." Concentrating upon the execution of those key tasks then ensures that the team remains focused despite the confusion around them.

General Warren clearly understood what the mission and its objective were. Amidst the confusion of battle, Lieutenant Hazlett understood them and their importance, too; he understood so well that he was willing to give his life for their achievement. They both viewed the unfolding battle before them through the singular filter of what must be done to achieve overall success. Today's business managers lack that overall view and the clarity that goes with it. They spend too much time striving to achieve poorly defined objectives and, therefore, don't have time to focus upon the actions that actually determine success or failure. As a result the organization becomes a collection of workers that mirror the signalmen on Little Round Top. Knowing nothing better, they continue to focus on the task at hand, relaying the next message, until it is too late.

Looming threats for today's managers may not be enemy soldiers creeping through the woods with weapons at the ready, but they are still there, lying upon their desks. Managers literally cannot see advancing disaster because of the trees that lie in their way. Those trees are reams of paper in a thick report of monthly statistics.

Managers will not find the answer or the solution to improving performance by burying themselves in those reports. Most of those management reports are filled with data—but very little knowledge or insight. They force management to again become like the signalmen at Little Round Top—just fight the fire and believe that the battle can be won by putting out more fires.

The solution is visible only from above the fray, only by stepping back from the minutiae of fighting fires. However, for management, especially for CEOs, there is no hill with a panoramic view and it becomes difficult to make the right decisions from ground level. Information is also filtered before it reaches them. Too often it is spun by those below them, shielding the bad news from those who need to see it. As a result, managers are often left without any understanding of what is really happening on the front lines of their business, problems go unresolved, and most employees just continue to plod through their daily work, waiting for the end of the day, then the end of the week.

Many executives do not even understand the necessity of stepping back and considering the battlefield from a bigger perspective. Sometimes, they misinterpret the need to have yet another meeting to get to the bottom of whatever issue is occupying their mind on that particular day as seeing the big picture. They believe, or hope, that they have a clearer picture of their company, the competition, the marketplace, and the future than those who work for them. In some cases they do, but too often they are mistaken.

What every executive seeks in a performance-challenged company is clarity—clarity as to why the company is not performing as it should, clarity as to what should be done about it. If the picture is distorted for the CEO, senior managers, and even middle management, it cannot be clear for those who work below them. When it is not clear at the tactical level, managers and employees revert to the age-old formula: put out the biggest fire first. Doing this makes perfect sense. If they don't put out the fire, it will burn down the building. They receive no direction to the contrary, and because it is what they have always done before, it becomes the norm. Without clarity, no one in the organization can know what is expected of them or how their actions affect the overall success of the organization. This does not mean the organization will fail or cease to exist, although many do, but the organization will never rise above a level of mediocrity.

The traditional response to this confusion is to hold company-wide or departmental meetings to get to the bottom of the problem. Because there is a lack of clarity on what the problem actually is, and what should be done about it, the meetings devolve into sessions where everyone wants to stay out of the glare of the spotlight.

The questions, even the answers, are repeated from company to company, in meeting after meeting, with only slight variation:

"Judging from last quarter, we have to do a better job. I want to know why we missed our goals and what we are going to do about it."

"We can't seem to get anywhere."

"We've done all we can. Now what do we do?"

"Why aren't we on course?"

## The Performance Puzzle

"What's wrong?"

Managers on the wrong end of these questions evade, seek scapegoats, offer excuses, and make promises they cannot keep. In searching for an answer, they give the typical ones: we lost that one big order, our vendors are raising prices, or we had to get those orders out the door so overtime was needed. . . . While stumbling about for a solution, managers again drag out the usual suspects: new sales incentives, new marketing and promotion programs, another mailing. They contemplate, even implement, workforce reductions, downsizing, right sizing. They parade out all the tired buzzwords and phrases: process re-engineering, balanced scorecard, efficiency studies, supply chain management, lean manufacturing, and data warehousing.

As the organization remains mired in this confusion, those responsible for determining the direction of a company, executives who realize how much the company is underperforming, are on a treadmill. They spend each month, every quarter, reviewing what has already happened, fixing blame, and ordering change—all things they have done before.

While executives and managers are stuck in this repetitive and frustrating cycle, each on their own treadmill, stuck in their own version of *Groundhog Day*, the market is changing around them, competitors are gaining ground, customers are leaving, profits are sinking. For management, the same beat goes on.

It is as if management is trying to solve a jigsaw puzzle without the picture on the box. They have no idea what the finished puzzle is supposed to look like so they use trial and error to figure out which pieces connect. Significant time is wasted and very often the puzzle never gets solved, performance continues to lag, and profit fails to grow.

Much of the frustration today's executives and managers experience comes from the tidal wave of reports and electronic spreadsheets that cross their desks. Their dogged determination to plow through these reports gives them the illusion of understanding what is going on, and they keep at it while holding out on the promise of a solution to their daily issues. With such a wealth of data, managers believe they should understand what is taking place, know what needs fixing, and grasp *how* to correct the problem. However, instead of offering answers, the endless stream of data only obscures reality. Instead of painting one picture of their performance the data paints many pictures, each seemingly equal in its potential to solve the overall puzzle. Managers perceive their company through a clouded lens. The future is always looming—distant, unknowable, and treacherous.

We found these same problems within our own company. We limited the potential of our own organization by viewing it only as a traditional accounting firm. Because of this, we could only attract clients who wanted specific, traditional accounting services. In order to grow and become far greater performers, we had to think of ourselves differently, perceive the market differently, and see the future of what our firm could become if we changed. First, we had to redefine our mission. Then we had to make sure we did the things necessary to realize this new future we had envisioned.

The result of this extraordinary evolution was that within seven years, our firm went from last place in our industry to first among our peer group. We got off the performance treadmill; we woke up from our *Groundhog Day*.

## THE MANAGEMENT CHALLENGE

Our firm was, in many ways, a prototypical organization that suffered from many of the ills of low-performing organizations. We lacked focus and insight into the market forces that were impacting our firm. We had no clear and convincing game plan to create the future we wanted. We lacked understanding of what was driving our performance and what could make us more successful. We made the decision to change.

Although dealing with these issues was a challenge, we found them easier than changing the culture that existed in the firm. All our partners were hardworking, but most worked on the wrong things—things that mattered more to them as individuals than contributing to the overall success of the organization. Most partners were comfortable with the status quo and were not really committed to or enthusiastic about making the changes a new future required.

We recognized this challenge as we visited various key partners. All were excited about the potential economic benefits of change, but almost all were cautious when the discussion turned to what was going to be expected of them. As we saw this unfolding, we became acutely aware of the need to reassure everyone that the new road ahead was not only exciting and desirable, but also did not threaten what they were doing.

*(Continued)*

---

**THE MANAGEMENT CHALLENGE** *(Continued)*

Not every partner came along easily. We recognized that we had to overcome resistance or we would fall short of our goals. That was just not acceptable. We decided to implement a training and communication program where key leaders met one-on-one with every partner. They explained what we were working toward and how everyone was an important part of the team.

At the end of the day, we learned that our partners were not really afraid of change. They were just confused about what change meant to them personally. We were convinced, by what we saw in our own company and in so many others, that people don't fear change if they understand the why and how of it. We worked to answer both questions. We were successful because we understood the challenge of change and met it head on and because we understood how to drive performance.

---

Solving the performance puzzle for our own firm required the same thing that each organization needs in order to achieve and sustain improved performance. Everyone at the top of the organization needs to see the big picture—one big picture—the same big picture.

Some time ago we met with a CEO and asked him our most basic question: "Do your senior managers have a clear understanding of what drives the success of your business?" Without hesitation and a bit offended by our question, he assured us that they did. Over the next few weeks, we met with all 38 senior managers and received a myriad of different answers to that simple question. When we presented the results to the CEO, he couldn't believe it. He deflated before our eyes and then became angry. "How could they not understand?" he yelled.

Why didn't his 38 key executives know what drove their business? It is a question that organizations spend significant time trying to answer. "How could this have happened?" is a question that consumes time during management meetings. The answer to that question, which has been sought by so many managers for so many long painful hours, is simple — it doesn't matter. Both the question and the answer do not matter.

The Performance Power Grid does not focus on how the performance puzzle came to be for those 38 executives. Instead it centers on how to change the results, how to get managers off their treadmill, and how to get the organization back on track. To a large extent, CEOs and corporate managers are victims of a system, not of their own making, but one in which they are forced to flounder, day after day, throughout their careers.

The solution to the performance puzzle *is* that picture on the jigsaw box. Once executives and managers, and even workers, see what they are creating, they can bring order from chaos. They can devise a plan that works. They can make progress each day toward their objectives. They can focus on execution. Systems can be set in place to focus everyone on what truly matters, on what drives the company toward uncommon prosperity. The fog ahead can be cleared away, and what were once stumbling blocks emerge as stepping-stones.

The Power Grid moves a company from the chaos of firefighting and confused, cloudy objectives, to an environment where everyone is facing the same direction, everyone is pulling on the oars in unison, and everyone is focused primarily on those actions that will drive the performance of the company beyond anything they ever imagined.

# CHAPTER 2

# The Impact on Power

**...**

In 1921 legendary golfer Bobby Jones, then just 19 years old, was participating in his first British Open. It was played on the St. Andrews Old Course, one Jones expressed his dislike for initially. Since bursting on the scene at the age of 14, Jones had quickly become the most popular American sports figure of his time. When he walked away from golf at age 28, two months after completing the first and only grand slam, rather than turn professional and play for money, the nation applauded his idealism. He remains a legend to this day.

On the third round of his first British Open, Jones was in the lead when his tee shot landed in the Hill Bunker of the par three 11th hole. The bunker is notoriously difficult because of the incredibly steep wall between it and the green. Rather than pitch back and keep his ball in play, which would mean taking a bogey,

Jones set his mind on clearing the bunker wall and landing on the green to save par. Five times Jones tried to pitch his ball out of the sand, five times it struck the wall and bounced back. No matter how unsuccessful his effort, Jones continued to do the same thing, over and over. With each stroke his chances for winning the prestigious British Open faded even more, but he doggedly stuck to it.

No matter how hard he tried, how much skill he brought to his stroke, the ball would not clear the wall. Finally, in disgust, Jones threw his club down, tore up his scorecard, threw it into the nearby river, and stalked from the course. To the jeers of the British spectators, he abandoned the competition.

Nine years later he came back to win the British Open, but toward the end of his life he called that day on St. Andrews an "inglorious failure"—the worst golfing day of his storied career.

■ ■ ■

Bobby Jones's dogged determination to do the same thing over and over, despite repeated failure, should sound familiar. It is par for the course in most organizations we see.

Companies, much like individual people, continue on the same path unless something happens that causes them to conduct business differently. Like Bobby Jones, even when profits are well below what is possible, they persist with unsuccessful strategies. Within these organizations, managers continue along well-worn paths, even though the same problems continuously arise, the same mediocre financial performance continues, and frustration grows. It only seems different to these managers because they are applying the same concepts over and over instead of literally striking a golf ball over and over.

## The Impact on Power

The question is: "Why?" Why in the face of continued frustration and persistently poor, or even mediocre, performance do managers constantly manage in the same way? Why do executives continue to think that the answer to solving the performance puzzle lies in a great breakthrough strategy, or in pushing the management team beyond their capability—believing they can actually change the very nature of who and what their employees are? Why does management continue on the treadmill, knowing that it leads nowhere?

The answer is in our genetics. In every aspect of human behavior, our natural tendency is to continue doing what we are used to, what we are comfortable with. Only when we are presented with a compelling change in our environment do we behave differently. This tendency, called *homeostasis*, is universal to all living organisms. It is so deeply ingrained within us because it is essential to survival. An amoeba will float about in a pond of water, taking in nutrition, multiplying again and again, until something happens that causes it to behave differently. For it to change, an external trigger is required.

Homeostasis applies equally to higher organisms. When we walk out the door on a bitterly cold day, or an extraordinarily hot one, our bodies will immediately do what they can to maintain an optimal state. Employees stay at jobs they despise rather than seek new ones, people remain in unhappy marriages, for much the same reason—resistance to change—until some compelling reason forces them to change.

It is easier, more predictable, and in a sense reassuring, to stay on the same path because at least we know it will get us where we want to go. Well-known roads, with their familiar twists and turns, are preferable because they allow us to navigate the known and require less effort. This allows us more time to think about or do things that require our immediate attention. For many of us, a vast majority of life is lived on autopilot.

That same human dynamic, manifested in so many aspects of our lives, plays out in the work place over and over. Employees park in the same parking spots each day, walk the same route to their office and purposefully avoid the same co-workers—every day. When you arrive at work in the morning do you open your e-mail before or after your first cup of coffee?

Managers conduct the day-to-day affairs of their office the same way and provide the same solutions for these same reasons. Their capacity to deal with problems is limited, and, therefore, they do the familiar because it requires less effort. There is nothing prompting them to change—to find better or more permanent answers. The root cause of problems goes undetected and the solutions make no lasting positive change. As a result, management and their employees are stuck putting out fires, often the same ones that just keep rekindling. Many managers put out fires from the very first day they are hired. In the end, most managers think that's their job—putting out fires.

Meanwhile this basic genetic resistance to change that each person has is contributing to the organization's overall resistance to change. There must be some stimulus to break each person, and the organization as a whole, out of old habits or the organization will never change to realize greater success. Once this initial change is achieved, there then must be a constant stimulus that prevents management, at all levels, from reverting to old habits until this new behavior itself becomes the norm. Without this sustained performance, improvement will remain as elusive as ever.

A few years ago we worked with a large, regional paint manufacturer. The company was making a profit, but revenue growth was stagnant. We were asked to help chart a path that would energize the company and move it beyond its mediocre performance. The metrics for success were simple: achieve positive revenue and profit growth.

During meetings with the CEO, we heard:

▮ My management team can't make a decision.
▮ Whenever we have meetings, no one shows any creativity and no one has any ideas.
▮ Our products are great but our sales team can't seem to sell more.
▮ Our profits could be better but we are only holding our own.

When we met with various members of the management team, we heard:

▮ The company has great products and an excellent reputation with customers.
▮ Profits are thin and revenue growth is stagnant.
▮ The CEO is too conservative and unwilling to change anything.
▮ Management meetings are a waste of time and focused on trivial issues.

How could there be such a disconnect between the CEO and the management team? In this organization, as in most, there was no underlying framework in place to unite the entire management team. Everyone was left to see the organization and its objectives through their own lens. There was nothing to provide a common understanding of the organization's actual objectives and what it would take to achieve them. Instead, in its place, they had an environment that created and allowed for excuses, poor performance, and risk aversion.

Over the course of time we learned that the CEO truly was risk averse. This CEO spent most of his time alone in his office pouring over spreadsheets looking for that elusive answer. We found that the management team lacked the courage to challenge the status quo. No one was leading and no one was following—everyone simply took action based upon his or her own perception of what was needed. There was nothing to unify their actions.

In the end we failed to convince the CEO that the answer to changing his company's poor performance was in the very nature of how he managed his company, and how his managers focused their efforts. This company is still in business. Its performance is still mediocre. The CEO chose to stay on his treadmill, and the management team, for the most part, chose to stand on the sidelines and cheer him on.

Contrast that organization with a very competitive discount software/electronics distributor. Their CEO was focused on making the company the best in its industry. She was inquisitive and open to new concepts. We spent time with her and her management team, really digging into their business and developing a strong understanding of what truly drove the success of their organization—the organization's *power drivers*. A structure was put in place that focused meetings upon these power drivers and prevented the minutia from draining energy and time. Ultimately the company grew to even greater levels of performance. It was sold three years later for more than the CEO ever believed was possible.

Most business environments, even two that seem as dissimilar as these two, are remarkably similar. They all deal with the same challenges: demanding customers, a changing workforce, decreasing margins, threat of globalization, rapidly changing technology, new competition, and most importantly, dysfunctional management teams. The answer to all of these challenges cannot simply be to tell management to change.

Traditional change management has been focused on doing just that for years, and has achieved surprisingly little success. The approach of traditional change management is relatively simple: explain to the management team that everyone resists change, explain how important it is to their success that they change, explain the benefits of changing and the drawbacks of not changing, and then, based upon this logic, *expect them to change*. Logical explanations in a sterile conference room simply are not enough to overcome homeostasis. For good or bad, we are not creatures of pure logic; we are prone to giving in to our emotions and make decisions that, to others who are not emotionally involved, seem nothing less than irrational. There must be something more; there must be something to cause change, and it must remain in place to prevent regression.

Over the years there have been many models that sought to change these dynamics: activity-based management, management by objectives, the Balanced Scorecard, supply chain management, *kaizen*, lean manufacturing, and Six Sigma (the newest model for improving performance), to name just a few. For the most part, they have not produced superior, sustainable performance in a great number of organizations. The number of failures far outnumbers the successes. They have not achieved these things because they rely upon the traditional change approach; they do not themselves change the way a company is managed and the way employees work. Each of these models uses a different format to present information—a format that is different than the organization is used to seeing and one that might even present different information than the organization had available before. However, none of them tie into the events that occur within the organization on a daily basis; they do not affect the focus and decision-making of employees at all levels of the organization. They put in place new philosophies yet fail to take into account the realities and the behaviors of the people who will have to read and use these new reports.

As different as each of the aforementioned management tools seem, they have two aspects in common: they all focus on changing organizational performance by changing the people as opposed to changing what they work on, and they all focus management attention upon the past as opposed to the future.

Remember IBM of the 1970s? If the company had been forward thinking it would have realized that the Apple desktop computer could only grow in power and application. Thousands of businesses that could not afford an IBM mainframe, the industry standard, could certainly afford a PC. IBM failed to see that the PC could replace the mainframe and wipe out its historical growth engine. Given its incredible versatility, there was only one direction for the personal computer: up. That left only one direction for the IBM mainframe to go: down. IBM was driving forward by looking in the rearview mirror.

Did IBM ever truly understand what was driving its success? Did it understand its power drivers? Did it understand, not what created its success in the past (the mainframe), but what would enable it to remain successful in the future? History shows us the answer: no. IBM missed one important business tenet—improving performance and creating lasting success is not based upon past history but upon those actions taken today that will lead to future success. The market does not accept past success as assurance that the future will remain bright, even for those organizations as successful as IBM.

This tendency is perhaps understandable. Remaining tied to past strategies is much easier for executives than creating a new way forward. The past is known; it is familiar territory. The future is a risk-filled mystery.

However, upon analysis, the future is not really as incomprehensible as it seems. Within any industry, most competitors are working from a similar position. A select few perform at a level above the pack; some remain one step from bankruptcy. The majority are struggling with the same issues. Those that figure out the best way to deal with them quickly soar to the top. Breaking out of the pack is not as difficult as it seems.

Breaking out of the pack, achieving strategic objectives, refocusing employees and overcoming the inherent resistance to change within your organization all require an understanding of what truly drives the success of your organization—your power drivers. Once the organization is heading down this new road or standing atop its industry, remaining there requires a consistent, daily focus on executing well in those key areas. The Performance Power Grid framework brings all of these different aspects together. It aids organizations in identifying their power drivers that link strategy to action. It puts in place a structure to continuously focus the attention of employees at all levels upon their achievement, while removing noise and creating clarity.

Perhaps even more importantly, the Performance Power Grid accepts a universal truth—people are not easily changed. Employees will continue to behave as they always have. Generally, they will not work as a team; they prefer to work within their own silo. They will not be guided by strategic objectives that lack substance and meaning in their daily life; they will instead focus on the tasks and issues that take up most of their time. They will not be guided by mission and vision statements, especially when they conflict with their own self-interests. The Performance Power Grid accepts these as fact and, instead, creates a solution that centers upon action.

In this way the Performance Power Grid becomes the underlying framework that connects all the dots in a cohesive, unifying fabric that reveals to the organization one clear picture. It uses the past to create insight into the future and gives management the tools and information they need to more effectively deal with it. It is both the initial trigger required to shift the organization toward greater performance and the ongoing stimulus needed to keep it there.

CHAPTER 3

# Harnessing
# the Power

···

On D-Day 1944, after he gave the order for the invasion of Europe, General Dwight Eisenhower wrote that he found himself with nothing to do. The units had been trained, the generals and men knew what was expected, and the enormous machine of the Allied Forces had been set in motion. From time to time Eisenhower checked on the situation and considered his next steps. While officers at every level beneath him were concerned with tactics, Eisenhower was free to consider the future. If the invasion was a failure, what orders should he issue? If it was a success beyond expectations, how could he exploit his troops' advantage? Considering alternative futures was an enormous luxury for Eisenhower, whose meticulous planning contributed to the success of the invasion and was directly linked to the eventual liberation of Europe.

■ ■ ■

General Eisenhower's experience has two vital lessons for today's managers. The first is the importance of strategic thinking. Eisenhower's luxury should be afforded every executive in every company. The higher the executive is in the chain-of-command, the more time should be spent on strategic objectives, on the future, and on making plans for what comes next. In most companies, CEOs and senior management spend little time on strategic thinking and way too much time on tactical, short-term issues and concerns.

Eisenhower's other lesson reveals how military strategy gets from the top of an organization to the bottom. Before D-Day, just as any time military orders are issued, high-ranking officers passed on Eisenhower's orders to their troops, along with the specific details of the mission that pertained specifically to their unit (the tasks that had to be performed). Each commander was required to add one additional section; they were required to include their "commander's intent." At each subsequent level of the command structure, the officer in charge relayed the orders and added his own commander's intent until the smallest, most specialized units got the message. This way, even if the command structure broke down during the mission, even if some units failed to do their part, even when all else went wrong, individual units knew what their commander wanted them to accomplish. Each unit could react to the rapid changes that were an inevitable part of warfare, and yet make each decision about how to react to those changes while keeping their eye on the bigger picture.

And so it should be in every company. It isn't enough to establish a reliable chain of command. Someone senior in the company must develop the strategic objectives and, in addition, the means of achieving them. Every level of the organization, from the boardroom to the cubicle, should know its part in accomplishing the commander's intent.

The inherent strength of the military model comes from not only its command and control function, but also its power to communicate. Two men in a foxhole know their job is to hold that position. They don't concern themselves with the artillery or tank units. There's nothing they can do about them, anyway. The tank units know what they have to do, as does the artillery. When each part of the whole performs its tasks as it was trained to, the army, the organization, will be successful. Like Eisenhower, executives are reduced to examining the situation map, focusing on the future and planning the next move. In business, the strategic planning process was designed to fill the role of relaying objectives, tasks, and intent. Unfortunately, it often falls short.

Strategic planning methodologies have been around for a long time, but they moved to a more formal structure in the 1980s, with the introduction of the Balanced Scorecard. Many companies found its promise of breakthrough performance improvement more difficult to achieve than they imagined because the true theory of the Balanced Scorecard received little more than lip service. It became a reporting tool that created little or no lasting positive impact on performance. Far too many companies simply populated their new Balanced Scorecard with the same tired metrics they had always used. They failed to view themselves through a new Balanced Scorecard lens and determine new metrics that would dramatically change their performance. Because most organizations never followed a process to determine what the new metrics should be and simply continued to use metrics they had always used, their performance never changed—as it shouldn't have. They never did anything different; they never changed their behavior. A new reporting format is not enough to break employees, or the organization as a whole, from the grip of homeostasis.

The problem with most strategic planning methodologies is that managers continue doing what they were already doing. Strategic objectives, which are entirely conceptual in nature, are not broken down into the new tasks and processes that will be required to achieve them. Therefore the connection between the concept and the daily workload of each employee is missed and nothing changes. The treadmill continues—the company's intent lost in another management fad.

The Balanced Scorecard and related strategic planning models are all traditional management models insofar as they are designed so that strategy remains the province of the top 5 percent of the organization. The people who actually make things happen on a daily basis remain out in the cold. These methodologies don't work because they solve only a portion of the performance puzzle—the strategy component. They forgot the more important part—changing the focus and decision-making of employees in their day-to-day work. They fail to produce *real, lasting* change because they fail to alter the individual's behavior.

To achieve sustained performance improvement, the process is actually fairly straightforward. Senior management defines the organization's strategic objectives, and, during that process, the objectives should be broken down into those that will drive revenue, profit, and customer value—the three true measures of success in business. (See Figure 3.1.) They must then ask a simple question: "What *must* we do to achieve each of these objectives?" The answer to this question is the first major principle of the Performance Power Grid. The answer to this question reveals to the management team their power drivers.

Power drivers are those critical actions that an organization must be good at in order to achieve its objectives and succeed in the marketplace; failure to execute in these critical areas will always yield mediocre performance. Because they are so critical to success, all employees should focus their day-to-day efforts on them, not via a conceptual linkage, but specifically on those

**Figure 3.1** Critical Organizational Dimensions

actions and decisions they make each day that have an actual impact on the power drivers they can affect.

Power drivers convert a strategic objective, something that lacks substance and is purely theoretical, into something that can be achieved. A company cannot grow revenue at twice the industry average or increase profitability by 5 percent per year. Executives, managers, and employees may wish for these things but they cannot *do* them. They can only take those actions that they believe will result in the achievement of these objectives. It is a cause and effect, action/result relationship. Therefore, it is on these actions, their power drivers, that they must focus their effort.

Typically, this translation of strategic objectives into actions or processes is the province of middle management. They are the layer that hovers between the boardroom and the cubicles, and because they reside in this limbo state, they cannot fully understand the "commander's intent" of their executives. Managers throughout the organization are left to make their own interpretations on what their department's or unit's role is. As a result some get it right and some get it wrong. Most simply do the best they can, do what they have always done, and continue to put out fires.

To overcome this problem, most organizations publish their objectives on intranet sites and in company newsletters. Although the logic of doing this cannot be faulted, it is faulty logic to think that employees at any level will take these into account when making decisions each day.

Even organizational power drivers, a relatively simple and straightforward concept in comparison to strategic planning, may never be understood by the organization at large, just as soldiers in a foxhole may not understand the strategy they are asked to carry out; fortunately they don't need to be strategists; that isn't their intent. Officers, the military version of managers, link conceptual objectives to the concrete actions that the soldiers must take to win the battle. The soldiers need to understand and perform those actions; anything beyond that is just a bonus. Their officers must be able to see, quickly and easily, how effectively those actions are being performed to ensure that the battle will be won. Each victory brings the organization one step closer to winning the war—achieving the strategic objectives.

Determining power drivers for each unit within the organization paints the entire performance puzzle for management, from the boardroom to the cubicle, from accounting and finance out to the edge of the enterprise. Strategic objectives are linked to the daily activities for employees in operations, manufacturing, and the back office, for the supervisors of assembly lines or shipping dock workers. This framework, the power grid, changes what employees focus on and prevents daily fires from distracting attention away from them. Without the power grid in place, management would revert to old behaviors.

We were recently at a conference on business performance management (BPM). More than 350 companies of all sizes were represented by mostly midlevel managers. These companies had already implemented one of the most popular change management models. However, their universal cry was that, after successfully implementing one of these many models, nothing really changed. By attending they hoped to gain insight into what they needed to improve their company's performance. Most left with no real answer.

When we left the conference, we asked ourselves: With all of these management models in place in so many companies, why hasn't performance really improved? The answer is twofold. Even if the organization was fortunate enough to understand what was driving its success, even if managers changed *what* they managed, they never changed *how* they managed. There was nothing to alter their behavior, show what each employee spent their time on, and evaluate how good or bad their performance was.

Consider again the military model. Objectives are clearly defined. Soldiers either win the battle or die trying. They take the hill, hold the bridge, or storm the beach. The objectives are real, concrete, and very clear. Modern business objectives lack this clarity. Managers spend the greatest part of their time in the dark about their part in achieving an overall objective. As a result, a company's energy and resources are dissipated. One department is trying to take the hill while the other is fighting to hold the bridge.

In the military model commanders get instant feedback and engagements have a beginning, middle, and end. In the heat of battle, commanders generally know what's working. When the battle is over, only one side has taken the hill. In business there are no clear winners or losers. Business never begins or ends; the battle is never over. This lack of clarity again calls for a framework that constantly focuses effort on what truly matters—on the activities that drive performance toward the achievement of strategic objectives—on their power drivers.

Managers need something that provides feedback on where the organization is now and where it is going in the future. Managers at each level must be provided a real-time view of what is happening. Just as General Warren did at Gettysburg and General Eisenhower did on D-Day, they must be able to stand back and examine the bigger picture. From the hilltop overlooking the battle-field, clarity emerges. This clarity allows each manager to make better, more informed decisions and maintain a focus on what is truly driving the success of the organization.

In order to achieve success, the organization must first establish for itself what success is. Internally, organizations define success as achievement of the strategic objectives set by management. These are the first steps on the path to greater performance. (See Figure 3.2.)

Regardless of business or industry—for profit or not-for-profit—all objectives should be focused on driving revenue, profits, and customer value. In all cases, if senior management cannot fit a strategy into one of these three categories, then they should reconsider even pursuing it. It may not be an objective worth achieving.

Many organizations have their objectives clearly defined and could quite easily align them with these three dimensions. If that is not the case for your organization there are many strategic planning

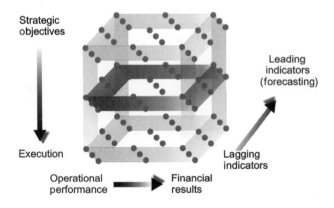

**Figure 3.2** The Performance Path

models to aid the organization in developing proper objectives. As each objective is placed on the appropriate dimension of the performance triangle, one question should be asked: "If I achieve this objective will it result in greater revenue, higher profit, or enhanced customer value?" The answer is not always as simple as it seems, but it is a pertinent question and one made for boardroom discussions. If the answer is no, the value of achieving this objective must be rethought. If unsure, the objective requires further clarification.

Once the strategic objectives have been determined, the next step is to determine the power drivers for each by answering a simple question for each objective: "What *must* the organization do right in order to achieve this objective?" The answers to these questions are the company's power drivers.

Take this thinking a step further. Ask which units or departments, including senior management, have the ability to affect the success or failure of each strategic objective. This creates a key association between actual units within the organization and actions that they need to focus on—again, their power drivers. (See Figure 3.3.) This grid work of unit and action associations reveals for the organization what needs to be done and who needs to do it. This is the foundation necessary to successfully drive performance.

Although this process allows the organization to understand what it should be focusing on, it still does not provide management with the feedback necessary to understand whether responsible units are actually focusing on what they should be. In order to do this, metrics are required.

Metrics serve as road signs for management. They let everyone know in which direction they are going and how far away the

**Figure 3.3** Determining Power Drivers

destination is. Properly constructed, they reveal where the organization is heading and give managers the opportunity to prevent failure or seize an opportunity before it is too late. Metrics are also that constant reminder that prevents the organization and the employees within it, at all levels, from slipping back into old habits. Properly used, they have the ability to directly affect employee behavior.

Metrics are custom-made for each functional unit. If staffing drives revenue, human resources knows that it must recruit, hire, and train the right number and type of sales representatives. The sales manager, who knows that an open slot must be filled quickly or else revenue will fall, acts to speed the HR process while taking other compensating action. Human resources and sales work together to reduce the revenue impact caused by vacant sales positions. At the same time, senior management might examine which sales regions have the highest turnover. Armed with that information, they too can work to reduce the impact vacancies have on future revenue. The entire organization, often without even knowing it, is unifying behind solving a problem that is draining revenue. Each individual employee may still *feel* as if they are working within their own silo, but feelings are not as important as taking action.

Traditionally, measures and metrics show what performance is, or even, sometimes, what it will be. However, this is only half the information that management needs. Knowing only what performance is still requires that management figure out why it is what it is, so that they can go do something about it. The Performance Power Grid fills this gap by explaining not only what performance is, or will be, but *why* it is what it is. This provides management with fact-based insight and prevents management from making decisions based upon prior assumptions and cultural bias. Placing this "actionable" information in the hands of those who need it allows them to take immediate action to improve performance. (See Figure 3.4.)

The power grid is not an academic exercise or a theoretical model. It has been applied with remarkable results.

A few years ago, FujiFilm USA set in place a management system that integrated internal marketing, customer service, and external business partners. The system resulted in a huge increase in customer value and was the first step toward a major revision of the consumer rebate industry. The company's ability to link customers

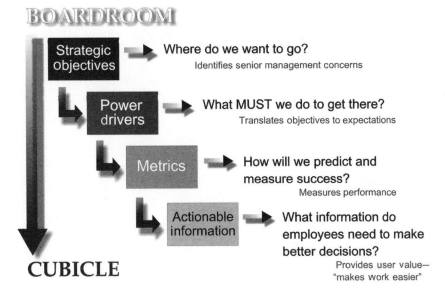

**Figure 3.4** Critical Performance Components

to sales not only provided better customer service and built brand loyalty, it allowed it to better target its marketing dollars. With the Performance Power Grid, FujiFilm USA found that it could more effectively predict its own future. It also helped generate sales by targeting consumers before they made repeat purchases, which may or may not have been Fuji products. All of this happened while the company maintained most of its original IT and e-commerce infrastructure.

At one of the world's largest pension funds, one valued at more than $20 billion, fund managers are responding to the needs of every one of its 130,000 clients around the globe every day. The fund now sees every transaction and knows the value of each participant's holdings, and it competently monitors daily fluctuations

41

in every currency in the world. None of these tasks could have been accomplished with their 30-year-old legacy system.

One of the major logistic corporations in the United States developed a system that analyzed the complex relationship between profit, customers, and the product's final destination. Although goods traveled through multiple carriers, passing through several company-owned facilities and delivered by one of six different methods, the company now knows immediately when something goes wrong. Not only do they see performance on a daily basis, but they also anticipate individual shipments that are likely to fail. They can spot underutilized trucks and anticipate how they can reduce expenses.

The process for reaching these destinations did not come from reading a textbook or installing a new IT application. For each of these organizations it was a journey of self-discovery, with the Performance Power Grid methodology serving as a knowing counselor.

When counselors work with patients, they've been down the road to recovery a hundred times before. After a session or two, counselors could simply tell their patient what needs to be done to turn their life around. Why do they stand back and let the patient struggle? Because a solution cannot be imposed; patients must discover it for themselves.

A counselor guides patients along a path familiar to the counselor, but one that patients only dimly perceive. The counselor gives direction only when the patients have clearly taken a wrong direction and seem unable to find their way back to the path.

At its core, the Performance Power Grid methodology acknowledges that an organization has its own personality and, therefore, its own personality disorders. That is normal. Unlike many other management models the Performance Power Grid does not try to turn a company into something it is not.

If success could be achieved by simply copying a good business model from another company, every company would be fighting for the lead instead of running with the pack. The Performance Power Grid must be done in your company, with your people, and in your marketplace.

---

**CHANGING DIRECTIONS**

Not long ago, we sat down with the director of branding at one of the largest consumer goods companies in the world. For the past year he had been investing considerable funds on a marketing/branding project, but his team of developers and outside consultants had made little progress. He was seriously considering canceling the project.

When we first met, the director's opening statement was that we wouldn't be needed for several months. We were to begin after the real work and reporting were completed. We spent some time talking about the problems he was facing and what he was trying to achieve. We discussed the course the project had taken over the last year and the lack of progress. We explained that what he was trying to achieve was possible, entirely possible, and painted a picture that helped him understand how it could work. We shared with

*(Continued)*

---

**CHANGING DIRECTIONS** *(Continued)*

him an approach different from that which he was currently taking, and the message resonated.

After two hours we had his approval to take over the project and move it along. We had listened and understood his problems. They were similar to the problems faced by most company managers, though to the branding director they were personal and unique.

The director intuitively knew a solution existed, that there must be a better way. He wanted to more completely understand his customers, people with whom his company had very little direct interaction. He wanted to meet their needs and sell more products. Intrinsically he knew that the enormous volume of customer information he was collecting could tell him all he needed to know. He was right, but he had no idea how to get there.

From past experience we knew it would not be an easy road to travel if he tried it on his own. There are landmines that are obvious to those who have been down this road before, but are nearly impossible for someone like him who was traveling down this road for the first time.

The company project manager was also part of the initial meeting and continually tried to steer us back to what they had been doing for the past year. At every opportunity she placed obstacles in our path. Fortunately, what we had to say just made too much sense.

The message was simple: focus on the things that truly matter—the things the company must do to achieve its objectives. Put the right information in the hands of the people who make decisions and put it there every day. Don't make them wait days or weeks. Give them information that can make an impact and let them know how they are doing. Don't force them to spend all their time figuring out what happened. Tell them what happened and why it happened. Better yet, tell them what is *going* to happen, both good and bad, so they can prevent failure and seize timely opportunities.

The value was obvious. For the director the traditional marketing approach to generating an additional sale of a $20 product was too expensive. The Performance Power Grid proactively and repeatedly generated one $20 sale, over and over, to individual specific customers, at virtually no cost. To him, that was priceless; to his organization, it was a competitive advantage.

Unfortunately, what is right or profitable today may be unprofitable tomorrow. Business just moves too fast. Therefore, the Performance Power Grid is an *evolving* model that constantly self-adjusts to changes in the marketplace and the organization around it. It leads managers into areas where they are missing something, where they have the wrong objectives, or where they have the wrong metrics. Because it evolves, it is not necessary to spend endless amounts of time devising a killer strategy or the perfect power drivers or metrics. If an objective isn't producing the expected revenue or profit, if the power drivers are not leading to the achievement of an objective, or if measurements aren't properly reflecting performance, the power grid will alert management.

Consider IBM's past performance in this way. IBM would have seen that the marketplace was shifting and focused on reexamining what was causing that shift. Internally the shift might have revealed that their customers were starting to buy extended maintenance agreements. If IBM had seen a disproportionate increase in maintenance income versus new-unit sales, it would have concluded that customers were hanging onto older IBM mainframes instead of investing in newer models. Customers might have signed another maintenance agreement to extend the usefulness of their IBM computer, biding their time before the maturation of the PC.

IBM's sales and maintenance staff must have seen PCs at customer locations. Did they report this information to their sales managers? Were they encouraged to? Did they consider it part of their job? Or, like the signal troops on Little Round Top Hill, did they ignore the enemy advancing through the woods?

Again, history tells us that within IBM no one who mattered was concerned. Officials were basking in the sun of success instead of focusing on the future and what was driving their business. IBM believed it was the computer industry. It believed its products determined where the market would go. Had it been looking at the right metrics and operating on the power grid, it would have known two or three years earlier that PCs were poised to devour its market share. It missed its chance and suffered the consequences.

When management isn't focusing on the right things, it is virtually impossible for employees below them to even know what they should be focusing on. Employees race about putting out fires; their vision is obscured by the smoke and chaos. They look to the past trying to understand how the fire could have started. It isn't their fault; they do want to do well, but nothing is pointing them in the right direction. Obviously, the fires need to be put out, but putting out fires leaves little time to improve the interior, build a new addition, repair the fire's damage, or fix what started the blaze in the first place. There must be something in place that allows for clear thinking and constant focus despite this chaos. Once in place and given some time, clear thinking and constant focus will make order from this chaos, and performance will continue to improve.

The technology behind the Performance Power Grid serves this purpose. It extends from the CEO's desk to the most remote workstation. At the top it resembles an executive dashboard, what is called the performance portal. Through the performance portal, management can see, whenever it chooses to, all the way down to individual transactions that are causing a problem.

For lower management and supervisors it is a simpler view that isolates key measures and metrics that they themselves can influence *right now*, and also allows them the ability to drill down to specific transactions that might be causing problems. In order for the performance portal to be important to each employee, it must contain measures and metrics that they are responsible for and ones over which they have control.

CEOs focus on summary information, a consolidation of everything below them. In the middle of the company, information becomes more specific, and further down into the organization, the consolidations become smaller and more granular until you reach the employees who focus most of their daily effort on processing single transactions (often one after another)—customer service, order entry operators, administrative accountants. A transaction is the single smallest grain of sand on the organizational beach. There are usually thousands of them. The technology behind the power grid brings it to life, rolling up information from the smallest suspect transaction into organization-wide trends. It reveals the picture on the jigsaw puzzle box so that everyone is working from the same view, toward the same view.

The metrics and power drivers displayed in the performance portal become a topic of conversation in every meeting—meetings no longer devolve into the blame game. The power grid, performance portal, and power drivers allow people to speak a common language. Workers from different departments can stand around a water cooler and talk about the things that matter most to the organization.

When the performance power grid is fully implemented, actions and strategic objectives will be linked. In the simplest form the power grid is telling everyone, "See this? This is important. Managing this is your job." It isn't about understanding strategic objectives, getting along with people, or even about how someone feels about her job. It is clear guidance about what is important and what is expected. (See Figure 3.5.)

Via the power grid, managers manage in a new way. They focus on the important areas of the business first and unify the ef-

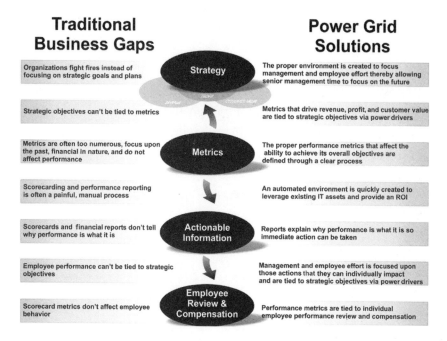

## Traditional Business Gaps

## Power Grid Solutions

Organizations fight fires instead of focusing on strategic goals and plans

**Strategy**

The proper environment is created to focus management and employee effort thereby allowing senior management time to focus on the future

Strategic objectives can't be tied to metrics

Metrics that drive revenue, profit, and customer value are tied to strategic objectives via power drivers

Metrics are often too numerous, focus upon the past, financial in nature, and do not affect performance

**Metrics**

The proper performance metrics that affect the ability to achieve its overall objectives are defined through a clear process

Scorecarding and performance reporting is often a painful, manual process

An automated environment is quickly created to leverage existing IT assets and provide an ROI

Scorecards and financial reports don't tell why performance is what it is

**Actionable Information**

Reports explain why performance is what it is so immediate action can be taken

Employee performance can't be tied to strategic objectives

Management and employee effort is focused upon those actions that they can individually impact and are tied to strategic objectives via power drivers

Scorecard metrics don't affect employee behavior

**Employee Review & Compensation**

Performance metrics are tied to individual employee performance review and compensation

**Figure 3.5**  Closing Traditional Performance Gaps

forts of people throughout the organization. When everyone in the organization is properly aligned with higher-level objectives, the whole engine begins to work properly, and at maximum power. This momentum, and the constant reminders of what is important, helps the organization shed bad habits. By providing clear information about what is important, about who is responsible for what, and about how each piece fits in with the whole, teams are built naturally, instead of trying to change the people themselves. Employees work together because, through the Performance Power Grid, the confusion and chaos are gone and the road map to success is as clear as the full moon on a crisp, cloud-less fall night.

The power grid may sound daunting, time consuming, even impossible. It isn't. It is like driving your own car to a new location. The vehicle is familiar, and although the landscape may not be, you are in the driver's seat with an accurate map, clear road signs, and a passenger who knows the road. Relax and enjoy the drive.

CHAPTER 4

# The Path to Power

...

**A**t its peak in the mid-1990s, the J. Peterman Company grossed $75 million annually. Launched in 1987, the whimsical catalog company carved out a profitable niche for itself, generating fierce customer loyalty. By 1995 it seemed to have it made when the highly popular television sitcom *Seinfeld* incorporated a parody of the company in the form of a real person by the name of J. Peterman. The episodes were some of the show's funniest. The exposure was worth millions in free advertising. Timing wasn't bad either. The show aired just as the company moved aggressively to open a chain of retail stores.

With the retail operation, CEO Peterman lost sight of keeping the main thing the main thing. What the company knew was catalog sales. What it knew absolutely nothing about was retail stores.

But the company needed to reduce its debt and the retail chain became its debt reduction plan.

"I had no perspective," Peterman freely admitted later. "What I should have done is said, 'We're going to slash inventory, overhead, and the number of items in the catalog.'"

The first retail store opened in November 1998. Ninety days later the company was in bankruptcy.

"When the ship starts to go down, there's nothing you can do. It takes on a life of its own," Peterman said. In 2003, he was able to buy his former company back for $1 million and is now slowly rebuilding the catalog business.

■ ■ ■

The path to improved performance is not paved with breakthrough strategies. One of the basic tenets of the power grid is that any sound strategy will achieve success as long as it is paired with superior execution. Conversely, the greatest strategy will fail if poorly executed. To create superior performance the proper mix must be a decent strategy, well executed. And the two must be connected.

Some companies spend a great deal of time and energy creating a grand strategy. What they call strategic planning is often, in reality, a budgeting and forecasting process. Many even refer to budgeting and forecasting as an enterprise performance management (EPM) or business/corporate performance management (BPM/CPM) framework. For others, strategy is just a vague, generalized, incremental restatement of what was done last year.

Look beneath what passes for strategy and you will typically find retreads of what the organization did before. Just like people, companies have belief systems that greatly influence their daily actions. These beliefs and myths are so strong that they color how an organization sees itself, how employees fit themselves into it, how managers behave, and the strategies they pursue.

When the Sarbanes-Oxley Act of 2002 became law, most accounting firms made no move to take advantage of it. Instead, their belief system told them that anything to do with public companies was owned by the Big Four accounting firms. Many smaller firms missed a tremendous opportunity. At our firm, we took advantage of Sarbanes-Oxley, and as a result we grew to over 100 professionals in a practice area that didn't exist a year before.

Strategy is like deciding what you want to be when you grow up. An early career choice is simply a goal, a target. If we are wise, we expect the target to change as we age. Likewise, strategies change as companies grow up.

We've learned that it doesn't matter *how* you identify your strategic goals. Use whatever method works best for your organization. In the end, the overall objective is to improve performance, grow revenue, increase profit, and enhance customer value. Don't worry about developing the perfect strategy. The best strategy is simply starting toward achieving superior performance.

Consider car manufacturers. Essentially they all want the same thing. They all want you to buy your next car from them. GM, Ford, and the others all share that same strategic objective, but they have different ways and means for achieving it. Successful automobile sales come from superior execution, not the uniqueness of the objective itself.

A company needs strategic objectives, but dwelling on what the right objectives are should not paralyze it. What matters is action.

One of our favorite questions to ask managers is: "What drives your company?" We've asked it of CEOs and managers across the country and this simple question has created some of the most interesting discussions we've ever had. Most managers tell us they had never before been asked to think about what really drives the performance of their company.

This is an important question for managers at all levels of the organization. Middle management and supervisors must be able to answer the question about their specific business unit. It is crucial. The answer is the key to their unit's performance. When their answer is in line with the organization's strategic goals, they are contributing to the organization's overall success.

A company's overall performance is a conglomeration of how well each employee (both managers and workers) performs his key function: processing a rebate transaction, handling a pension claim, or moving customer goods on time. In order for the individual and company to succeed, everyone must perform their key functions well.

Take the example of a supervisor knee-deep in the minutia of loading or unloading trucks, approving overtime, reprimanding tardy employees, and granting vacation time. In the midst of all this, anyone could easily lose sight of the goals of the company. However, something needs to be in place to keep the supervisor focused on what drives the success of the company. If that focus is lost, a supervisor's day degenerates into fire fighting. Every manager must realize that a supervisor's real job is not putting out fires. It's making the organization successful. It's focusing on the organization's objectives and power drivers. This is the purpose of every single employee in every single organization, but that purpose is rarely felt.

## The Path to Power

All power drivers start with the company's objectives. Objectives cascade from the top of the company through the divisions, departments, units, and individuals. From that mosaic of objectives come the power drivers, the actions that lead to achieving the company's objectives.

We mentioned earlier that we consulted with one of the largest pension fund organizations in the world. It had already established objectives and metrics and was comfortable with them. We accepted these objectives and set in motion a process to develop and implement the power grid around those objectives. We first determined the power drivers for each objective and then the metrics to measure them. Finally, we implemented the technology that brought the grid to life.

When the fund managers began operating within the power grid they discovered that a key customer value objective was simply wrong. So wrong, in fact, that it had nothing to do with helping them support their customers. They further discovered that this erroneous objective had been consuming a disproportionate amount of management time.

The reason we accepted the pension fund's stated objectives was because, at its core, the power grid is an evolutionary process. If the fund's objectives were wrong, the grid would reveal it. In the end, that is exactly what happened—with little fanfare and no externally imposed change, they realized their own problem. With us as counselors, they were able to find, quickly and easily, a solution to their problem.

Each element of the fund's power grid was not perfect at inception, but when something was incorrect, it became apparent, visible, and so obvious that a better solution became easy to implement. We also knew when the fund was losing focus, because their performance, via their metrics and the performance portal, told us. When this happened, the affected unit, as well as the individual employees within it, realized the problem and made self-adjusting corrections, with little senior management intervention or input. The focus was always on what was truly important.

Pension fund managers, like managers in most organizations that go through a clear analytical process that ties strategy to action, discovered that identifying strategic objectives and power drivers was difficult. They were often hindered by the myths and assumptions that had accumulated over the years. These myths acted like anchors, dragging down performance-improvement efforts. Few believed that a different future was even possible; those that did, didn't know how to bring it about and couldn't lift the weight of the anchors alone.

Myths often control behavior throughout a company much as they do in our personal lives. Self-image is either a catalyst spurring us to greater deeds or a weight dragging us down. An organization's behavior reflects its collective self-image, and its self-image was developed over many years by managers' preferences, customer perceptions, and employee attitudes.

Managers develop an at-work belief system based on company history, experience, and dealings with their bosses, other managers, and employees. Their beliefs eventually affect their expectations and lead to the creation of myths, all bubbling up to affect the way employees behave and interact at work. This process is aided by each manager's tendency to work within isolated cubicles and silos. However, corporate mythmaking is not confined to the mid-manager level. Big Blue was living a myth by believing it was the computing industry. We know where that led it. Moving a company's performance above its current level is challenging because it is encumbered by all the negatives of belief, expectation, myth, and isolation. The key to breaking this cycle is to accept these things as part of doing business without fighting them. Instead, expend your effort (another limited resource) on getting everyone to focus on the right things, regardless of how they feel or what they believe. This new focus will erode myths over time; coincidentally it will also reveal those myths that were, in fact, based upon truth so that, in time, they too can be overcome. Once power has been applied to the grid, managers often find that they feel as though they are still working within their own silo and that nothing has changed. As counselors guiding them through this process, that feeling and maintaining the illusion that nothing of substance has really changed are exactly what we want.

For the vast majority of people, change creates fear. Fear creates increased resistance to change and an endless cycle begins. This prevents an organization from improving performance because it is associated with change. The power grid methodology allows employees to emerge from their own silos when they are ready. In the end, they do not resist the change because leaving was their own choice. All the while, the power grid itself is focusing everyone on what really matters—their actions. It is providing all involved the information they need, and making their jobs easier. It is the difference between giving someone a shortcut to avoid traffic delays each morning and suggesting they avoid the delays by coming to work an hour earlier—one makes their lives easier and the other asks that they actually change. There is no question which they will welcome and which they will resist!

Organizations often get caught up in the desire to change employee feelings and to gain their buy-in. It is a noble effort and one that feels right. However, what the organization really wants is the end result—improved performance. It isn't necessary to take this circuitous route to reach that final destination. Changing what employees focus upon first allows the organization to improve more quickly. If, as a manager, you really do feel that you should take the noble stand, then consider this approach from a different perspective: improved performance is considered success in almost any organizational environment; success reduces stress; less stress makes people's jobs and their lives happier; they feel good—noble result achieved. The only difference is that this approach is more likely to actually achieve some tangible result.

How does this work in real life? Recently we had the opportunity to work with one of the largest student educational training corporations in the country. We began by participating in their annual management three-day strategic summit. We were asked to assist in helping them set the course for the company over the next year and a half. The first night we worked to gain an understanding of their perspective on the future. We then spent the next two days assisting them in developing strategic objectives and the means to achieve them. We also discussed cultural influences, such as myth making, which, if left unchecked, would continue to hold back company performance. We wrote a long list of company strengths and weaknesses on whiteboards, scattered about the room.

There was an undercurrent of suspicion and distrust that ran across the pages. It was so obvious that once the words were put up there in black and white it was undeniable, and also unavoidable. The CEO of this company had a strong personality and was committed to the goals he believed in. In his mind he had a clear path for achieving each of them. As a leader he was not inclined to listen to others whose goals might be different, or to consider other paths toward their achievement. He didn't care to talk about power drivers and implementing the power grid methodology, although he was supportive of this approach. We knew that most of the management team members thought it was important to get the issue of the CEO's inflexibility on the table, and solve it in some constructive way.

We challenged the management team to examine each of its objectives through a revenue, profit, and customer value lens. One area of heated discussion was the optimum revenue mix for the organization. The CEO's very strong opinion about this was contrary to just about every other member of the management team. The second major area of discussion had to do with the CEO's management style. As he was ignoring their ideas, managers wanted the CEO to see that he was acting like Custer when he brought the Seventh Cavalry to its death at the Little Big Horn.

Once these interconnected issues were on the table and after some heated discussion, we stopped them and asked a question: "What do you think will have the greatest impact on your success and the company's long-term profitability: the revenue mix or how well you execute the strategy?"

Their conclusion was unanimous: execution trumped objective. They knew they would never get there if things continued as they had been in the past, and so they all felt they could grow either way, if they could all get on the same page (although the degree to which they would grow was still in contention). This agreement meant that managers and the CEO had to let go of some of their feelings and beliefs. The personal need to win had to die. Coming to this enlightened conclusion highlighted another key fact. The CEO's style of management was secondary to the real issue of how well the company executed its strategic objectives. Because there was no agreement on what the strategic objectives should be, there was extra room for negotiation and disagreement about how to proceed, instead of a clear focus on how to achieve the objective itself.

Although neither group was right or wrong, both sides realized that it was wrong to let the organization flounder over an issue that was preventing them from succeeding. Which strategic objectives to pursue was a business decision. In this case it was going to go the CEO's way or no way at all; his personality simply would allow for no other outcome. However, taking the objective down to clear actionable steps and specific measures for which groups or individuals were responsible put the company back on track toward greater performance.

This does not discount that each manager within this organization had to make a personal decision about whether they wanted to continue to work for this specific CEO. His style was not going to change. Through one-on-one discussion with managers we found that, by and large, they simply wanted to do a good job and feel that they were contributing to the organization's success; that is all that most employees want. Having a clear goal and a clear path to achievement allowed them to focus on their area of responsibility, the things they took pride in each day.

Implementing and then managing within the power grid shifts thinking away from fuzzy logic. It emphasizes clear thinking and a focus on the actions that are required to succeed. One of the biggest drains on energy in any company is looking into the past to figure out what went wrong and *who is to blame.* Knowing what went wrong or who was responsible is important—to a degree. However, in most business environments it takes too much effort to figure it out and that process itself can be very destructive.

These dynamics often cause management effort to be wasted on the blame game and on another popular sport—the staff meeting. We once worked with the CEO of a printing company who excelled at draining organizational energy. Every day he called his managers into his office to yell about the day's problem. The managers all knew what he would say next. During this daily ritual, they nodded as they took their licking. They then wasted the rest of the day chasing the CEO's crises. The long-term effect of this charade was an organization that never rose above mediocre performance.

The meetings this CEO held constantly reminded us of the *I Love Lucy* episode where Lucy pretended to know Hollywood stars that she didn't actually know. When Lucy dressed up like Harpo Marx to fool a nearsighted neighbor, the real Harpo dropped in. Lucy moved in wordless unison with Harpo, mirroring every movement of the famous comedian. To an outsider this is exactly what the company was doing. After each staff meeting the printing company's managers would go back to their departments and imitate his actions, derailing the entire organization.

An alternative to *I Love Lucy* meetings is to keep the organization's attention focused on strategic objectives that improve revenue, profit, and customer value. This seems difficult and confusing, because revenue, profit, and customer value are often considered boardroom-only topics of conversation, but they really are not.

There are only three ways for any company to grow its revenue: increase prices, increase customers, or sell more to existing customers. That's it. Consider profit, the second leg of the triangle. A company can cut expenses or increase revenue. Those are the only options. It is often made more complicated than this, but in reality it isn't.

Customer value is more complicated. Why does a customer buy from one company over another? What makes one product more appealing than another? What advantages does better service give one company over another? The answers to these questions are where customers find value in a company. In the end they must translate into revenue, and eventually profit. (See Figure 4.1.)

Virgin Atlantic Airways Ltd. has done a superb job of defining and improving customer value. On a recent flight from the United Kingdom to the United States we were picked up at our London hotel by a Virgin Atlantic limousine and taken to the airport. The driver called ahead to report the number of bags and arrival time and then drove to a separate section of the airport garage with a special Virgin Atlantic office. Once there, a Virgin employee took our bags and gave us our boarding passes. Airport security was there to check our documents. There was no waiting in line. We simply walked to the airplane where the most comfortable sleeper seats ever invented were waiting. Any of 50 different movies were available for viewing by each passenger, at any time. On top of that, the food was as good as that served in any quality restaurant.

This was Virgin's standard service for first-class customers, a status we attained because we were allowed to use our frequent flier miles for an upgrade. Virgin elected to give first-class passen-

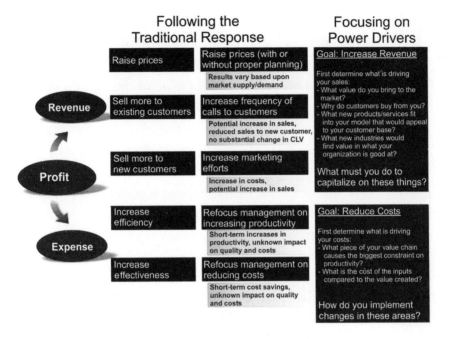

**Figure 4.1**   Overcoming the Traditional Approach

gers extra value in order to differentiate itself from its competitors. From our experience it worked!

Virgin Atlantic paid attention to customer value because the costs of flying are not infinitely adjustable. Material, production, shipping, and marketing costs tend to even out over time. Cutting them would not provide much in the way of a sustainable competitive advantage.

However, remember the importance of execution. If Virgin Atlantic does not execute properly, their costs may not be sustainable. If they gain too much of the first-class market, the competition may begin adding the same extra services too. Virgin must

65

constantly assess customer value, make adjustments to stay ahead, and execute better than other airlines. If they fail, the market will catch up to them, and eventually they will lose their customer base and the added revenue and profit that goes along with it.

At some point, a group of executives within Virgin came up with this customer value-oriented strategy. A wordy document probably exists somewhere explaining it; it may even appear in mission or vision statements posted throughout company facilities, but it ends there. Just a few days after these new posters were put up, employees stopped noticing them; they became wallpaper. The objective itself does nothing for the majority of the organization and may largely be misunderstood.

To Virgin's credit it understands that it isn't critical that employees understand the intricacies of corporate strategy. Customers on the other hand, must constantly feel its presence. It is each and every employee's job to do those things, to take those actions that will cause customers to feel it. Those are the things that *must* be done right to achieve success and to give their conceptual strategies the power to drive the market in a beneficial direction—their power drivers.

CHAPTER 5

# Focusing the Power

...

Navigating the small winding streets of Hopatcong, NJ in an 18-foot bucket truck was never easy. Cars lined the narrow streets, eager pedestrians waited on every corner, each one waiting to jump out and cost you a few weeks' pay or your job for their injury. Fortunately the heavy rain had blown out the night before, but Ron still couldn't find 331 Bucknell Trail. You'd think they'd use the global positioning unit (GPS) in this truck for more than just counting the number of times we stop for coffee, he thought. The map was no help and half the roads were closed for the one-year sewer project that had been going on for the past 36 months. Unfortunately dispatch was no help either. Call in for directions, get too much attention, the saying went among the union linemen. Besides, if he asked dispatch they would just tell him George found it pretty easily the day before, why couldn't he? He suspected they wouldn't even hide their sarcasm.

George did find it, but the irony was that he had blown the assignment off and closed the job with a false failure code that placed the fault outside the building. It was a strange coincidence that outside the building was also outside George's job description.

So he kept searching. The minutes ticked away and his productivity continued to drop. If this kept up he would be in jeopardy of not getting his three jobs in for the day, three jobs being the currently agreed upon number he had to complete so the supervisors would leave him alone. He could do three jobs by noon if he really wanted to, but not when this happened. He'd find the house eventually and then the real fun would start.

Like George, he too had a job description. He was supposed to work only outside the customer's house. Shaking his head, he knew what had happened. George probably went there, couldn't find the trouble in the line easily, and closed it out because he didn't want to crawl through the attic, fish a wire up a wall, or fight off a few dogs—could have been anything. To avoid getting hit with a repeat call, he closed the assignment for outside repair, and left the outside repairman with no choice but to do it himself.

They all knew how it worked, and they all knew how to work the system. When the inside worker didn't want to finish a job, or had something better to do with his time, he closed the job for the outside repairman, even though the problem was inside the house. When the outside repairman arrived he was prevented from closing it with the proper code, an inside code. If he did, when someone had to return to complete the job again, a repeater got logged against them. Someone else had to go back and repeat the work he already did, and this would get logged in his file. It might not hurt him now, but if something serious happened in the future—if he crashed into one of these cars right now—it would come back to haunt him. That left only one solution—finish the job himself.

Inevitably, he'd have to discuss his low production for the day with his supervisor and take the heat. Perhaps, after work, he'd discuss it with George, but for now, there was really nothing he could do to change it.

■ ■ ■

One of the reasons most organizations perform poorly is their lack of focus on the daily tasks that help them achieve the key objectives of the organization. Most of the daily effort is expended on activities that add little or no value to the achievement of the organization's objectives. Employees may be busy as bees, like Ron in his bucket truck, but their actions too often do not provide any lasting benefit.

Imagine, instead, a company where all that talent, training, experience, and energy is focused on the activities that drive success in the areas that really matter: revenue, profits, and customer value. Imagine every small decision helping the company achieve its strategic goals. It sounds like fiction; unfortunately, for most organizations today, it is.

However, it should be and could be happening in every company. Creating those dynamics is the main purpose of the power grid. People should be focused on the key actions that they can affect. They should be performing the key tasks that drive them toward the company's objectives. Pyramids were built using only pulleys, ropes, and a strong, unified purpose. It's a lesson we've learned with

71

manual labor, yet one that largely escapes us in modern corporations. The Performance Power grid brings these things to reality.

It is a manager's job to create unity of purpose. The CEO must unify the entire company just as individual managers must unify their own departments. Too many companies are managed via planning meetings, issuing reports, creating policies and procedures, and disciplining when things don't happen. In addition, these types of management activities create a gap, a *missing link*, between strategic objectives (what the company wants to achieve) and the tactical decisions (tasks or activities) that are made each day. That gap is as vast as the distance between the boardroom and the cubicle. Power drivers bridge that divide. (See Table 5.1.)

By utilizing the power grid and its unifying power drivers, management is able to tell the organization, "This is what is important." Managers are able to tell specific employees, "This is what you are responsible for—see these stoplight indicators? Stop them from turning red—stop us from failing." People understand immediately that this is the focus of their job. Clear definition removes confusion. It adds clarity to daily activities. No longer can an employee say something isn't their problem. If the light is not green, it's their problem. They better do something about it or be prepared to explain why.

At lower levels our approach seems overly simplified and based on common sense. It has to be. In any company, most people do not understand strategic objectives. Continuing to waste resources trying to change this lack of understanding is just that, a waste. It is better to simply show them what it is their job to do, give them the information they need to do it right, in real time, and light their way to success.

**Table 5.1**   Proper Focus of Critical Components

| | Position | Proper Focus |
|---|---|---|
| **BOARDROOM** | Board of Directors | Fiscal performance, corporate governance, Sarbanes-Oxley compliance |
| | Executive Management | Fiscal performance, corporate governance, Sarbanes-Oxley, strategic objectives, external influences, market/industry metrics, forecasting performance |
| | *Power Drivers* | **THE MISSING LINK BETWEEN STRATEGY AND EXECUTION** |
| | Middle Management | Objective achievement, tactical performance, vendor/partner/distr. performance, actual to budget performance, key leading indicators |
| | Front-line Management | Tactical performance, actionable transactional information, current and leading indicators |
| | Knowledge Worker | Tactical performance, actionable transactional information, current and short-term leading indicators |
| | Line Worker | Tactical performance |
| | Vendor Partner Distributor | Key performance reporting, Internet portal interfacing |
| | Business to Business Customers | Portal interface |
| **CUBICLE** | Business to Consumer Customers | E-commerce |

Every manager has seen moments when action aligns with intent—a "momentary unifying factor." It frequently happens when the boss sets a last-minute deadline. A major customer is considering going to a competitor if something doesn't happen. In crisis

73

mode, the boss grabs whoever is needed and they all work to-gether to get the job done—no matter what needs to happen or whose responsibility it is. For that brief moment, people emerge from their silos and work together toward a goal that they can all understand.

As good as it was to work together and accomplish something worthwhile, the unity brought about by this momentary need dissi-pates. As quickly as they unified, employees quietly return to their silos and it is business as usual. This is the reason why strategic re-treats rarely result in meaningful, lasting change. Once the excite-ment of the planning session passes, people revert to behaving as they always have.

The absence of a momentary unifying factor impacts productiv-ity. For Ron and George, the telephone workers in our story, accept-able productivity was arbitrarily decided between management and the local shop steward. Management agreed that if each worker did three jobs per day, that would be considered acceptable perfor-mance. The head of the local union went along. Three jobs a day were easily achieved. Drivers could still stop for coffee and an after-noon snack. It was a win-win, even though in the bigger picture the company was the loser.

If Ron or George needed to go home early, the supervisor would say, "Not until you finish your three jobs. If you finish them early, you can punch out." Not surprisingly they would then get the work done early. If they were able to do it when they wanted to, isn't it fair that management expected them to work at that pace every day? After all, the company *needed* the work done just as much as employees needed to go home early. But this common sense expectation rarely occurs. Few supervisors are driven by the need to raise productivity above the accepted level. Demanding higher productivity automatically causes conflict, and conflict is something most people avoid.

The power grid increases productivity without causing conflict or fighting human nature. Instead, it takes the counselor's role and presents work functions in a less aggressive way. The power grid allows change to happen naturally, behind the scenes, without personal confrontation. When management clearly states what is important to the organization, what units and employees are clearly responsible for, it is much more difficult to fight the system. It is clarity of purpose, responsibility, and result that reduces confrontation, confusion, and conflict.

There is a general belief that employees fear accountability. This is true only when viewed through the lens of most business environments. Employees fear being accountable for things they are unaware of, until called on the carpet for them, for things they cannot control, or for things they do not understand. Employees do want to know what they are responsible for, they want to know what their performance is, why it is what it is, and how they can affect it to make improvement. By and large, they want to be given the freedom to make decisions about things they are responsible for, and to make the improvements they see possible. Under these conditions they do not fear accountability; they actually don't even consider it accountability.

When employees make improvements in the process they work with each day, they typically do it because it makes their jobs easier. They aren't implementing process improvement or complying with the principles of change management; they are simply making their jobs easier. Similarly, by taking this approach, the

Performance Power Grid sidesteps most change management issues and simply makes their life on the job easier.

A logistics company we worked with provides a number of lessons in avoiding confrontation. The company had a union work environment similar to the one Ron faced, but it handled labor/management issues through the power grid.

One of the logistics supervisors created a large whiteboard attached to the wall in the start-of-shift meeting room. Each morning the supervisor updated every route number with the name of the route driver, productivity from the previous day, the numbers of stops completed, the average number of stops for the week, and their on-time delivery percentage. The drivers were surprised to see their numbers. Performance varied widely, often for good reasons such as miles between stops and dense traffic areas. These are things the route drivers understood and could justify in their minds. However, for some drivers, productivity was low—often embarrassingly low.

In the beginning the supervisor gave no details about the numbers, just explained what they meant and noted what they were. Beneath the union bravado, most of these drivers were just regular guys who took a measure of pride in their work. They were also very competitive. Although as a group they lived by the union principle of resisting even the most minor changes, to avoid public embarrassment, many of the worst drivers improved their performance without any mention of it. Overall, productivity increased. Drivers even began teasing each other about their performance during the morning start-of-shift meeting.

A few weeks later a management-friendly fill-in driver requested one of the senior drivers' routes during vacation week. The supervisor agreed. During this one week, the fill-in driver doubled the productivity and service performance on this route. That driver's performance was a topic of much amusement among the drivers. When the regular, more senior driver returned the following week, he wasn't amused; to him it was very personal.

The supervisor sat down with this senior driver and explained how supervisors were judged on performance; the supervisor's performance was essentially the summation of each driver's individual performance being written on the board each day. He offered the senior driver a choice: improve his performance to a level that had been demonstrated was easily attainable or lose the route to the more capable driver. In order to avoid the embarrassment and discomfort of losing his regular route (not to mention his upcoming holiday tips), the senior driver improved his productivity. This set a new standard for the driver group and again raised the overall performance of the group, without any driver/supervisor confrontation beyond the everyday norm.

The message to the entire driver group was clear: productivity was important to management. Those who didn't pull their weight would lose their route. The result: productivity increased without an increase in hours worked and again without confrontation or resentment. This is what the company wanted. Their main customer value power driver was on-time delivery. Their main profit metric was increased stops per hour. They achieved both through the power grid. Now multiply that through every other unit in the organization. The power grid provided the knowledge, the visible insight into what was important, and how each driver was doing both against the objective and against one another. Human nature did the rest.

We worked with another company, one providing services in a nonunion environment. There, management wanted processing time to improve. As part of its implementation of the power grid, a performance portal was created that showed how each employee was doing in comparison to every other employee. For the first time the processing department had the information it needed to understand how it was doing and what was causing success or failure. With it, the processors could take action to improve performance. The processors never thought for a moment that they were being forced to change or told what to do. To them they were just doing their job—a job that was easier now.

The supervisors involved had their own performance portal. They spotted failure before it happened and had time to shift workloads before it was too late. They could also tell which workers were best at processing certain types of cases. They held meetings to acknowledge top performers and asked these employees to discuss their best practices. Employees were helping each other improve case processing time. It should come as no surprise that the single most important power driver to the company was case processing time. It accomplished this while realizing a return on investment and no resistance from employees.

Initially none of the employees in these companies understood the strategic objectives management was trying to achieve, or even most of the power drivers. Again, they didn't need to. Employees in each unit within each organization understood the actions they were responsible for and the measures lit their way. Those actions were their power drivers—the actions that led to the successful achievement of strategic objectives. Understanding their jobs this way allowed all employees to do each day what was necessary to keep their unit on target and on track toward the company objectives.

All that is required is for each worker to understand what he or she needs to accomplish in achieving their unit's objectives. What does Ron, or any telephone lineman, need to do to help his unit succeed in the telecom industry? They need to complete as many jobs as they can each day without another worker coming in to redo their work. That is how they can have the most impact on their company's power drivers that are aligned with profit and customer value producing objectives.

In order to ensure that Ron does what the company needs, he must have a supervisor who monitors all the unit's key actions (monitoring performance via the metrics in the performance portal). It is the supervisor's responsibility to ensure that all issues and problems affecting Ron's ability to effectively and efficiently perform those key actions are fixed quickly and proficiently—and permanently. On the surface, this seems fairly simple. "I need you to complete three jobs a day. Fix them right the first time—no repeaters." However, real life is more complicated than that for the supervisor.

Ron's job description also says he must treat customers politely, work safely, operate his vehicle and equipment properly, and obey traffic laws. His supervisor's responsibilities are much broader: juggle union slowdowns, contract violations, worker complaints, discipline letters, truck maintenance, vehicle collisions, lost and stolen tools, days off, sick days, holidays, floating holidays, and driver no-shows. How much hope is there that Ron's supervisor can teach him the complex strategies of competing in a telecom industry? None.

Fortunately the supervisor doesn't need to address that question. The power grid handles those details by providing knowledge (useful information) to the right person, at the right time, and at the right level of detail. It is focusing the supervisor's effort just as effectively as it is allowing the supervisor to focus her employees' efforts.

The power grid recognizes that most people choose to work within their own silo, or in Ron's case, his own bucket truck. The grid doesn't fight this tendency. Instead, it works with it. Power drivers that involve multiple units create a common understanding of shared goals and teach interdependency. Over the course of time this naturally draws people out of their silos, or cubicles, or trucks, as they realize that they personally can be more successful with the assistance of those around them. They each begin to focus on the same problem from their own perspective (the perspective of what they are responsible for and what they can affect), but they are each working toward a common goal that is in the best interest of the organization. Isn't this the very definition of the teamwork every organization seeks?

In reality, both Ron and his supervisor want the same thing. Generally speaking, they both want to be successful at doing a job that is no more difficult than it has to be. If they were entirely creatures of logic, it would be simple to sit down and explain to them that, if the supervisor makes the worker's job easier, then that will actually be making the supervisor's job easier too. They truly are interdependent—they both must be competent at their individual jobs in order to be jointly successful. Chances are that if they were pulled aside and told this, they would agree that, yes, they are interdependent and need to work together. However, once they were back out in the work environment, with its conflicting goals, roles, and priorities, their interdependency wouldn't be tangible enough to constantly keep them on the same team. There needs to be something in place that accepts this reality, removes the conflict, and makes their interdependency tangible.

The power grid does this by getting Ron to understand what he is supposed to do, the actual tasks he should be focusing on, and what is expected of him. It then provides a way to measure his performance and show him why his performance is good or bad. That's enough for Ron to know. There is no need to lay siege to his bucket truck until he buys into the team approach. It is unlikely that Ron is ever going to use a performance portal, or any of the technology behind the grid, but his supervisor will, and that creates the common language that both of them need to communicate effectively (just as it does between a manager and an executive or even between a worker and an executive). It is a language that focuses both parties upon the important tasks, processes, and responsibilities, and presents factual information that can be discussed, analyzed, defined, or even redefined. Once this language is in place it serves as a starting point for both of them to learn and grow together. As they discuss the day's performance, the worker can explain the things that caused him trouble (made him less efficient and effective). As their relationship grows (as they become a team), the worker will often explain not only what the problem was, but how those problems could be solved to improve performance. For the worker, this is the supervisor making the worker's job easier—not something he is going to resist. The supervisor gets the improvement in performance that is critical to her success and the success of the organization.

Few organizations have a common language with which they can discuss performance, but imagine the power of bringing each piece of the organization together to discuss improving performance. This is merely a side benefit of managing on the grid.

Part of what makes this approach so successful is the immediacy of the feedback that the supervisor gives the worker. Under typical business environments, where feedback is delayed until reports are generated and distributed, supervisors cannot approach their subordinates with specific information about their performance until after they have both moved on to the next business problem. It is difficult to then go back to employees and ask them to recall and improve upon something that happened too far in the past to recall specifically. The problem can be too easily dismissed by either party because it is no longer relevant to where they stand *today*.

Once a company begins managing on the power grid, silos and other barriers break down naturally. Employees are compelled to emerge from isolation. The shared language and the *process itself* builds the team. Just as it was once in an employee's best interest to work in isolation, the proper focus causes a new work behavior to emerge. It is now in the employees' best interest to work together.

This approach does not require significant change in terms of how people work; they simply work on different things. It fosters change in a nonthreatening way. What occurs is a change in concentration. It isn't so much that Ron was doing the wrong things before; it is far more likely he was doing too many things and giving them the wrong priority. The power grid did not change Ron's supervisor, move walls, or realign the organization. It's all about focusing attention on the things they can control, those things that have the most impact upon achieving the company's strategic objectives.

Just as improving performance is about focusing and getting employees to interact, so, too, is the process of figuring out what they should actually be focusing on. We conclude with an example that highlights the need to observe the process and listen to employees who are actually performing the processes while putting the power grid in place within an organization. Those employees often already know the solution.

A client in the promotional products industry was having problems getting the right products to stores in time for each buying season. In order to achieve a quick win during the early stages of implementing the power grid, we focused our initial attention on two departments: forecasting and purchasing.

Employees responsible for forecasting were judged on their ability to accuracy forecast the quantity of products that customers would purchase. If they forecast a high demand for a product and no one bought it, they were in trouble. Conversely, if demand became high, and there weren't enough products to meet that demand, they were also in trouble. They considered accuracy to be their power driver and didn't concern themselves with the overall company objectives. They were focused on doing their jobs well. At the completion of each ad campaign, usually a year later, they were rated on the accuracy of their forecasts and the amount of overstock. As you would expect, they focused all their effort on ensuring top performance in this area.

Employees from the purchasing department often visited the forecasters to prod them to complete their forecasts as soon as possible. Purchasers were eager to have the forecasts in order to finalize their buying plans. The purchasing department was focused on timely delivery of the product from overseas. They considered the on-time delivery of these products their power driver. They had to ensure that products were available to fulfill customer orders. The sooner they received the forecast, the better chance they had of ensuring that the products for an ad campaign would be in stock.

During our discussion with employees from both groups, they made it clear why things were the way they were. The purchasing agents knew that the forecasters would receive negative evaluations if their forecasts were off; the forecasters knew that the purchasing agents would take the heat if the forecasted products were unavailable to customers. However, despite this knowledge, in the end, each department's employees were most concerned about their own performance. There was no teamwork, just enlightened self-interest.

We discovered that the problem wasn't that their power drivers were wrong, they were incomplete. It was understandable that they didn't take the time out of their day to contemplate the overall strategic objectives of the organization, but they were wrong not to have taken the time to understand the objectives of their own organizational unit—something that should have much more impact on and be much more tangible to each employee. This is a common problem when employees work in isolation.

When drawing out the impact of the forecasting department, we saw that they impacted the customer not in one but in *two* ways. Certainly, they had to accurately forecast product demand (which affects both revenue and profitability), but they could also impact the customer by not completing the forecast in enough time for purchasing to even get the product in stock. We reasoned that it was only by combining these two power drivers that the impact of the forecasting department could be measured accurately. (See Figure 5.1.)

These changes eliminated the isolation of the two departments. Power drivers and metrics were now shared. The departments had to work together to determine what products should be ordered. They weren't *physically* working together, but they were working to achieve the same goal. If forecasting was looking at a product that purchasing knew was difficult to obtain, the submission date of the forecast would change. If forecasting knew a certain product was going to be a hot item, but purchasing hadn't even ordered the product, forecasting would give purchasing more lead time. The forecasting employees were now judged on a new level of performance. The new power drivers gave the company

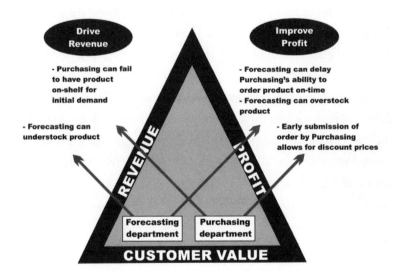

**Figure 5.1** Determining Unified Power Drivers

what it wanted—the right products sitting on the shelf when customers placed an order. Over time, as forecasting and purchasing learned more about the larger process (the process that actually connected the two different departments), and they were able to talk about things in a common language, they came up with an even better solution. They created "partial order dates" based upon overall demand. This allowed them to purchase some of the hottest items well ahead of time, getting a lower purchase price while ensuring stock availability, and then make the final increases to demand by the final forecasting deadline. This increased the overall accuracy of forecasts, improved on-time delivery, while also improving profitability.

The success of the power grid comes in part from not trying to change the spots on a leopard, just as it did not substantially change purchasing or forecasting. The departments still had the same employees doing pretty much the same thing they had always done. What was different was their focus. The two departments now worked as a team, even though they were independent, self-contained units.

By adding a second power driver and metric, we changed the definition of success. That change also changed the behavior of the forecasting department; it caused them to make different decisions. From the overall organization's perspective, these were *better* decisions. They were driving revenue, profit, and customer value, even though they never knew it. That is the power of a metric.

CHAPTER 6

# Measuring the Power

▪▪▪

When Apollo 13's oxygen tank exploded it caused instruments onboard the spacecraft and at mission control to give readings never before seen, even during practice scenarios. After the fuel cells shut down, the crew shifted to emergency batteries to preserve enough power and oxygen to give them a chance at survival. Among the many problems they were dealing with was the lack of power to reboot the navigation computer. They needed the most basic thing—a guide through the vastness of space. As Hollywood made famous, they placed planet Earth in the dead center of their porthole and used this as a means to measure their re-entry. When everything else failed, this simple trick allowed them to measure their progress toward their target—home.

■ ■ ■

A car, or an airplane, has a dashboard. It lets the operator know where he is, the direction he is heading, and the status of each key system. On every road and highway, there are signs to let drivers know what is coming up ahead and how far they are from their destination. Every sports event has a scoreboard to let the teams and spectators know what the score is and how long they have left to change it. Early seamen used the stars to determine their position on the open seas. The astronauts of Apollo 13 had a dashboard, but widespread system failures took that away from them. In order to survive they had to invent a new means of measurement. Keeping the Earth within view through a port served as their new dashboard. This simple technique allowed them to measure their angle of approach into the atmosphere and gave them the feedback they needed to constantly adjust and stay on course, to stay alive.

Over and over, all around us, we see mechanisms that provide constant feedback to keep people informed about where they are and where they are going. Yet within most business environments, such constant and timely feedback is absent. Lacking are the key tools that tell whether a unit, department, division, or even the entire organization is moving toward its objectives.

Managers need this guidance. For most, even the most basic measures that are needed to tell managers if their organizations are accomplishing their missions are lacking. However, the need itself still exists, just as it does in most aspects of our life. With the power grid, metrics and measures serve this purpose. Properly used, they have the ability to focus effort and influence behavior like no other modern business tool.

To fill this gap, most companies measure the past and then attempt to use it as a guide to their future destination. This is a very natural tendency because the past is what we have the most information about. From financial reports to IT systems, numbers are all about the past, yet managers spend little time using historical data to understand future trends and likely outcomes.

Once an organization has its strategic objectives and has identified its power drivers and each unit's ability to affect them, there needs to be a metric to measure that relationship. In the end, metrics, and the associated actionable information that explains their "why," are the only pieces of the performance puzzle that will have substance. They will appear on the dashboard of the performance portal for each manager or unit who needs to know what they are and who can then influence them. There is no need for people within the organization to see a metric over which they have no control. This will serve only as a distraction, a potential fire that draws their attention from those key actions that the organization needs them to focus upon in order to succeed. These are actions that they *can* influence. The power grid always seeks to minimize distraction and, therefore, gain the most concentrated focus by all employees. It is a basic approach that should influence every aspect of the grid.

Remember the logistics company and the supervisor who displayed driver performance on a meeting-room whiteboard? If that supervisor had a metric that said he must load and dispatch 35 trucks before 9:00 A.M., it must be within his power to do something about it. He might need to change some of the procedures for handling loads, modify start times, or add personnel. In order to create the proper dynamic between expectation and outcome, to be held responsible, he must have the power to influence it. If he does not have the ability to affect it, but is still held responsible, this supervisor will be forced to create a work-around that gives the appearance of success but typically violates a company policy or procedure. When this is eventually uncovered, the supervisor will be held responsible for this violation without the root cause, the inability to affect an outcome, ever being addressed. Thus, through that small interaction, the organization will remain on the treadmill.

As the only piece of the performance puzzle that has substance, it is essential that metrics measure the *right things*. Just as they have the power to focus effort upon the right things, they can focus everyone throughout the organization on the wrongs things. Just as they can change behavior for the good of the organization, they can instill bad behaviors. This is why the process behind the power grid starts with objectives and power drivers, not with existing measures. If the organization simply automates existing measures and reports, nothing will change. There will be the expectation that change will occur, just as most organizations implementing the Balanced Scorecard using their old metrics expected change. Unfortunately, change will not happen. Why? Because management will have failed to change both *what* they managed and *how* they managed it. The power grid changes how managers manage; the measures within the individual performance portals change what they manage.

## Measuring the Power

One area that is measured by virtually every profit-driven organization is sales. (Not-for-profits typically have salespeople too, but they pursue funding. Funding is actually revenue, even though it is often not thought of as such, and the same rules apply. Revenue and funding both allow an organization to continue offering its products or services.) Sales are typically one of the easiest areas to measure. Most companies have a set sales plan, clearly defined sales growth objectives, and compensation plan metrics that are reviewed almost every day. It is the one metric nearly all company management teams share, and it often dominates all other metrics and objectives. However, sales metrics are usually established based simply upon wishful thinking and hopeful optimism. They are rarely based on a meaningful and honest examination of the marketplace and a company's resources. They are largely influenced by the corporate myths previously mentioned. How many of the businesses that go out of business each year budgeted bankruptcy-producing negative growth?

It isn't unusual in any organization to find that at the end of the month sales are usually off plan. After spending countless hours poring over IT generated reports, a sales manager calls the sales staff to find out why. "What happened and what are we going to do to catch up next month?" It's as if demanding better sales will make it happen. Every month, the same worn-out excuses are offered to explain the negative sales variance:

- "Our customer was close to pulling the trigger on this big order and now it looks like it will be next month."
- "Our order fill rate was really low this month, which cost us a lot of sales."

▐ "Competition is really tough out there and pricing is becoming a real issue so we had to discount heavily to book
sales or risk losing customers."

There isn't a manager around who has not heard one of these
excuses and become lulled into reacting to it or, worse yet, into
accepting it. The one reliable result from these standard answers
is a continuation of what was done in the past, possibly with some
minor tweaks. No real changes are made to the sales program, behavior, or tactics; therefore, the future results are almost always
the same.

In order to improve sales performance, managers must understand what portion of the sales process is falling short. Because
most managers do not know *why* sales are off, it's only by luck that
they ever stumble across a solution. This may sound harsh, but an
honest examination will reveal that pinpointing the real reason for
a drop in sales is rarely done. Many organizations find it extremely
difficult to do.

This difficulty arises because they are focused on the wrong
things and fail to view the sales cycle through the proper lens.
Sales are a result; sales revenue is a result of the sales process being
effectively executed. Management cannot simply ask for a better
result and expect to get it. Sometimes they will get it, because
some salespeople are good enough to figure out how to get new
sales on their own. Most salespeople will simply work more hours
doing the same things and, therefore, close more deals or sell more
product. These actions may create a short-term incremental

growth in sales, but they will not produce sustainable, superior sales performance. By and large, most salespeople are not good enough to go out and increase sales by 15 percent over prior performance without organizational support and a new approach. (See Figure 6.1.)

Imagine the same scenario for a company operating within the power grid. First, there is an accurate estimate of the marketplace. Company leaders have established objectives and drivers. Where the company intends to move is based on true and effective analysis. Management takes the time to understand how each sales objective is to be achieved. What are the drivers that result in achieving each objective? What actions will maximize each power driver? Finally, effective and realistic measures are created. This ensures that managers will always know where the

**Figure 6.1** Painting One Picture of Performance

company is and where it is supposed to be going. Managers see their performance *each day*, and are shown exactly where they stand as of that day.

If sales are down, those with a need to know go to their individual performance portals. Very quickly they can see which step or steps in the process are underperforming. They can drill down into these metrics to understand what actions have been ineffective. The nuances of each organization's sales process vary, but the process itself will typically be the same. Is the organization reaching the market? Is the market finding value in its product or service offering? Are they overpriced (or underpriced)? Has a new competitor changed market dynamics? Is the real problem sales to new customers or a drop in repeat purchasers or customer lifetime value? Is the organization failing to properly fill the orders and causing higher returns or order cancellations after the fact? And none of these questions yet touch on whether sales are the real problem; perhaps it is really profitability.

With a few simple clicks of a mouse, the performance portal points to the problem and tells them why they are having that problem. Managers can now spend their time figuring out what to do about it, deciding what tactics are not working, and implementing real changes to the sales process. Managers are focusing on the cause of problems, not trying to affect a result; they are taking action, not focusing on results.

Performance portals are specific feedback devices. Each layer of management will have a portal that deals with appropriate areas of responsibility. Metrics become more global the higher up in the organization it goes. CEOs, for example, will have performance portals that deal with broader, company-level objectives. Shipping supervisors will have portals that deal only with the metrics appropriate for them.

The supervisor's manager will see the supervisor's metrics as well as his own. A supervisor knows the manager is aware of what the metrics say about performance. Managers will soon want to know what the supervisor plans to do about problem areas. Under pressure, but with information, a response to a negative metric takes place at once, without a meeting, telephone call, or e-mail. And the response occurs while there is still time to get back on plan.

Measuring against a plan enhances the significance of a metric. Within the power grid, a plan is a target or goal. Monthly sales, direct labor percentage to sales, billable hours, and new customers are metrics that grew from plans. If actual results show that a metric is on plan, managers should spend little time examining that objective. In those instances where the company is below plan, all affected parties can drill down through the specific metric within a performance portal to determine why. Once managers are armed with a real understanding of why things are wrong, specific actions can be taken to create better future results.

Companies that are above plan have a tendency to celebrate and relax. A more effective response is to understand *why* sales are above plan and ask, "Is there something taking place we can take advantage of to drive sales even higher in future periods?" Or, "Is there something that we have to do to make sure we meet this increased demand and still provide superior service?" Imagine the power!

### THE UNITED NATIONS

With the United Nations, the concept of creating a performance-oriented environment was perhaps more revolutionary than anywhere else. As a multinational organization, the environment was more political than most. Proper conduct was a major factor in career advancement.

At our first off-site planning meeting, 20 midranking managers and executive officers had probably already been told by their bosses not to commit to anything without consulting with them first.

The meeting leader was politically savvy and we made fairly quick progress in only a few hours. We had the indicators on the board, prioritized, and narrowed to four key initial metrics. We broke up into four teams with one indicator per team. Each group's job was to determine how their indicator should look, what calculations were necessary, and what the planned performance values would be.

The group discussing the first indicator struggled with it for quite some time. Eventually they discovered that it had no performance value; it didn't actually prompt any action. This indicator, which measured the resolution of compliance issues generated by oversight board audits, called for the audited department to simply report the status of a compliance violation, not address the issue or fix it. If nothing had been done to remediate the problem, reporting that it was still open met the requirements. How could we improve performance if meeting the standard had absolutely no impact on achieving the goals of the organization? Changing this indicator would be the first small step toward performance management.

That afternoon the group went around and around, attempting to figure out different, fancier calculations to fix the problem. They kept putting more and more information on the screen. Then someone asked the question: "What if we do what these metrics are asking us to do—will it help us achieve our goal?" The answer was, no.

Then someone dropped a little pebble in the pool: "What we really need is a due date." Someone replied that would probably fix the problem. "The policy is the problem," they joked, but there was no way this group was changing the policy. "But why can't we change the policy?" some unknowing outsider asked. That brashness brought a huge laugh and broke the ice enough to get the ball rolling.

The conversation picked up. Then clarity emerged: "By simply putting a plan value in, like when do you expect to resolve this issue, we could influence the policy." In the back of everyone's mind was the realization that they would be the ones to set the due dates and then be held to them. However, that was the original plan: let the people who will be

*(Continued)*

---

**THE UNITED NATIONS** *(Continued)*

responsible for success have a hand in creating it. The new policy was helping the organization achieve its overall mission by doing the right thing. "Due date" was added to the whiteboard and the joking began. "Guess I finally have to paint that musty wall," said one member. "Guess I better start locking the safe," said another. "Guess I better stop the kids from losing the keys to the front of the main building," added a third.

When we gathered again with the main group, the entire room was quiet as this new metric was presented. It was a small change, the smallest of ripples, but that little group had set something in motion. It would take time, but eventually it could change one of the most influential organizations in the world.

---

This is the advantage of allowing management's attention to be guided by the performance portal, the indicators within it, and their associated stoplight colors. At a glance, these red, yellow, or green indicators show management where they need to focus and which problems, or potential problems, need their attention. Those who have never operated within the power grid inherently believe they should focus upon the red indicators, red meaning that you have already failed or are off plan. However, those who have managed on the grid quickly understand that the true areas of importance are those metrics that show yellow—an early warning that failure is approaching. Yellow tells the future and allows management to take action in time to prevent future failure or to realize a future success. In this way, management takes action to produce a desirable result—before it is too late.

For most organizations it will seem impossible to see and affect the future in this way, but it is one of the most powerful cultural shifts that the Performance Power Grid will create within the organization. The performance portal has the ability to show trends and to take into account future actions that still must occur before a customer can be satisfied or before an objective can be reached. When the performance portal becomes a crystal ball for the organization, the real power of the Performance Power Grid hits home. (See Figure 6.2.)

There are also a few tricks to ensure that the crystal ball remains working properly. If a metric always reflects good performance, it should be questioned. Is it important? Is it measuring what we think it is? Perhaps it was set up incorrectly or the target is too low. It is the same when an indicator is always red. The perfor-

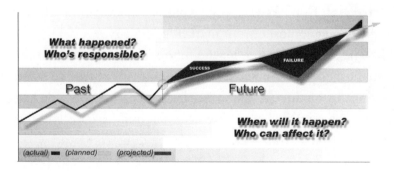

**Figure 6.2** Seeing the Future

mance bar might be set too low or too high. If a metric stays red or yellow for an extended period of time, it will eventually be entirely ignored. If it is ignored, then it is not having an impact on performance and should be removed or redefined. Over time, the crystal ball will adjust itself to the constantly changing reality of your organization.

Try this exercise in predicting the future. Draw a line on a sheet of paper that illustrates your company's sales growth for the last six months. Smooth this line out and it becomes your baseline. Now extend the line forward into the future. Use the historical data to predict the next six months. If nothing changes, this is where you will be. The only way to move that line up toward greater success is to take action now. You must start taking action now that will produce the results you wish to achieve in the future. At the end of those six months, it will be too late.

Be careful. We once worked with a company to drive their sales. One day a sales associate came in grinning broadly. The CEO asked, "Why the smile?" The associate crowed that sales for the first six months were up almost 15 percent. Although happy with that, the CEO said that the industry-wide sales increase was 20 percent. Don't look at positive metrics in a vacuum. Place them in the larger context of your market or industry.

The same holds true for the future. If your sales are declining, you must *do* something to change it. If not, eventually you won't be selling any product. As a business leader, you must be able to easily see what is actually happening *right now* and have insight into *why* it is happening. Your focus needs to be directed toward what isn't working.

## Measuring the Power

This is, in essence, what we mean by managing the future. The problem for most companies is that they lack the measurements, the insight, the objectives, or the skill to pull it off.

The performance portal is what brings the power grid to life and allows it to succeed where other approaches have fallen short. Within the portal are those things that management has deemed important to each employee within the organization. The portal does tie these things back to conceptual strategic objectives, but it translates them into specific actions or processes that pertain specifically to the employee looking at his or her own portal. All the confusion of boardroom talk, mission and vision statements, and company newsletters has been set aside, and in its place are 10 to 15 metrics for each employee that they themselves can affect and are responsible for. To each manager's or employee's delight, these metrics tell them not only what they are responsible for, but what their performance is, and *why* it is what it is, in a way that actually makes their jobs easier.

It is because of these dynamics that metrics can actually change employee behavior and influence their decision making. Consider the salesperson who was asked to go out and sell more in order to improve revenue. Because most salespeople have some influence over the pricing of their product or service, they affect more than just revenue. If the correct power driver for this salesperson were determined, they would also reflect their ability to affect profit. If a profitability metric is added to those that the salesperson is responsible for, and this metric then shows the salesperson which sales were and were not profitable and which will and will not be profitable, her behavior will be affected. If salespeople are aware that their performance will be judged based upon both revenue and profitability metrics, they will be more inclined to approach the sale differently, set pricing at different levels, or discuss the opportunity with the appropriate operations or service manager. By showing salespeople a bigger picture, their behavior will start to change. If the profitability metric is tied directly to their compensation, their behavior will most surely change—quickly. (See Figure 6.3.)

It is easy to assume that salespeople will consider profitability in their decision making, and certainly many salespeople do, but management does not *know* if they are actually considering profitability. With this metric in place, assumptions and the unknown are set aside. In the process, the organization has begun to break down age-old barriers that often exist between sales and operations. Employees leave their silos because it is in their best interest. This is how the power grid sidesteps the tradi-

**Figure 6.3** Driving Desirable Behavior via Power Drivers

tional obstacles to change that are present in every person and every organization.

Although tying metrics to employee compensation is the final and most influential way to affect employee behavior, it should be done only with metrics that have been in place for at least a short time. When a company first implements the power grid, it is not unusual for some of the metrics to be wrong. The metrics could be measuring the wrong things or the objectives on which the metrics are based could be wrong. It could even be that the metrics have become inaccurate and are not picking up changes in company performance.

The better the power drivers, the better their relationship to specific units, the more exact the metrics will be. However, because the power grid is self-adjusting, you should not get hung up on creating the perfect metrics—just get started. It will help you understand where the metrics are wrong.

Consider the business model of our client who organizes and sells products at school book fairs. They worked with the local PTA and school principal to determine a sale date, time, and place. On sale day, company employees arrived with a truck full of books already packed in movable display racks. Based upon their consultations with the PTA, company buyers knew how many buyers to expect and the number of books to stock. The company took care of everything. Proceeds are paid by buyers directly to the school and the school returns the company's cut back to them. The process is so simple that if the PTA, principal, teachers, and students are happy, the company will surely be invited back.

In order to grow revenue, one of the company's strategic objectives was to increase the number of book fairs. In order to achieve this objective, its power drivers were:

- Develop new, and maintain current effective relationships with PTA and school decision makers.
- Make book fair events simple and easy to execute.
- Ensure that high-demand titles are always available.
- Price events to ensure profit for each school.

All of the company's metrics were derived from these power drivers and their relationship to specific units within the organization. How would sales create effective relationships? How would operations ensure the event was simple and easy from the school's perspective? How would contracting and purchasing make sure hot titles were always on the shelf? How would finance create a model that was attractive to the school but still allowed for sufficient internal profit? The organization's ability to focus on these critical actions each day, to see its progress toward them, and to quickly and easily understand when things were going wrong were what got it to the top of its industry.

In 2004, when four hurricanes swept through the organization's headquarters state and destroyed over 60 schools, the customer base around its main office was devastated. Because they were managing the future, management saw very quickly that there was no way they would make their year-end revenue goal. Because they were managing on the power grid they could quickly take action to improve revenue in other areas of the country. They offered additional incentives to schools that booked new or additional events; they offered bonuses to the sales department. They moved high-demand inventory to other regions, ensuring higher sell-through percentages and cut overtime in their home region. These were real actions that would help increase revenue and improve profit. Instead of waiting to see how bad the damage would be at the end of the year, they took action.

Had they only asked sales to go out and schedule more events or had they just asked operations to move inventory and cut overtime, they would have been managing in the traditional manner. That is how most companies manage—gather in a huddle, call a new play, and then everyone back to their positions to run the play. Meanwhile, business is constantly moving. This company made these changes to its daily plan and brought them into the power grid. Management changed the power grid to reflect their new environment. In the performance portal they changed specific plan values for sales, inventory, and overtime metrics to show upper management and individual managers whether they were executing against the new standards. Their environment had changed— they changed with it. That's managing on the Performance Power Grid.

CHAPTER 7

# The Power of *Why*

▮ ▮

In 1968 the Army Reserve was a way for young men to fulfill their military obligation without risking combat duty in Vietnam. However, for eight weeks, those on their way to Vietnam and those in the Reserves who were due to go back home after training went through basic training together.

After two weeks of training at Fort Leonard Wood, Missouri, Company D had become known as a bunch of goof-offs. The college-age reservists in the company did not really care how well they performed. Why should they? They would be civilians again in a few weeks. Why bother getting all worked up about this soldier stuff?

Three weeks into basic training the reservists decided that of all the drills, bayonet training was the most ridiculous. They listened and watched the drill instructor show them how to fight with a bayonet. They were instructed to yell and grunt much like the fighters in a Kung Fu movie. They were separated into two-person teams to practice bayonet fighting. It seemed so foolish that many of them started laughing, turning the training into a game.

After a few minutes, the drill instructor (DI) screamed at them all to stop, put their bayonets away, and sit on the ground. Once the men were down the DI didn't scream or lose his temper. He said simply: "You guys think this is real funny? You wise-ass college guys think this whole Army thing is a big joke. Any of you who are not here as reservists stand up. [About 25 percent of the guys rose.] Those of you who are sitting look around at the ones standing up. Let me tell you something. Most of these guys are going to 'Nam. Most of them will be scared. They'll have to spend nights in jungles and do things they never thought they would have to do. There will be a time for every one of these guys when the bayonet training they are getting here will save their lives. So go ahead and laugh and have a good time, but remember, it's not funny for these guys standing."

That was it. The DI walked away. The group was stunned. For the first time they understood why they were doing what they were doing—and the reality hit the reservists like a ton of bricks. Without another word they all rose and practiced bayonet drills as if their lives depended on it. They saw the big picture. They knew they weren't there to goof off but to train as if their lives depended on it.

At the end of basic training, there was a review parade, and awards were presented to companies for top performance. Company D won just about every award there was to win—they understood *the power of why*.

**■ ■ ■**

*Why* allows us to understand. It provides purpose. It provides one of the most critical elements of employee performance, understanding the importance of what they are doing, not in the context of some overall grand strategy, but how what they personally are doing adds to the ultimate success of any entity's purpose, be it winning a battle or creating profit.

It provides insight that allows employees to take action. It unifies effort and energy in a way that reduces delay and increases results—a key relationship within dynamic business environments, industries, and markets. When the question of *why* goes unanswered, each employee must view the answer through his or her own personal preferences, bias, and agenda. Even with the best intentions, this fragmentation prevents the organization from focusing on what truly drives its performance. The power grid prevents this by answering *why* on two levels: for each individual employee and for the organization as a whole.

On a very broad level, the power grid and the performance portal have the effect of telling everyone what the CEO or senior management team regards as important. They then pass the "commander's intent" down the line, telling all subsequent managers and units what is, therefore, important to them and what must be focused on. The system makes *why* institutional. Everything is connected—the objectives, the power drivers, the metrics. All are aligned. If it's on the performance portal, it's important. Why is it important? "Because it's in the portal." For day-to-day work, that is reason enough. It is not necessary to make employees understand everything or to provide the big picture. The message of the power grid is simple: "You play an important role in our success. Do these things right to help us succeed."

The message is not about strategic plans. Rather it is: "Manage these things well." In its simplest form, management is telling everyone in the organization: "When the light turns yellow, do something about it. That's your job." Through the power grid, management's message and objectives are effectively delivered to every manager and worker in every cubicle in the organization, in terms they understand and relative to their own position. Over time, each manager and employee will come out of their own silo, join the team, and see the big picture—when each of them is ready. They all will change when they choose to change. In the meantime, the grid is getting them to do what the organization needs to have done, regardless of their personal feelings.

That is on a broad scale. Although these things are what allow the organization as a whole to achieve and sustain superior performance, they are, by and large, still intangible. It is the power of *why* that individual managers or workers, sitting in their own offices or cubicles, feel that will truly drive improved performance.

## WHEN POOR PERFORMANCE IS ACTUALLY GOOD

Each Thursday night during an engagement with one of the world's largest freight forwarders we would have dinner with a leading district manager to discuss his scorecard and analyze his district's performance. When he arrived late one night, one of us asked what he had accomplished that day. "Nothing," he replied, obviously tired and frustrated, "absolutely nothing." It was the third Thursday of the month and the monthly scorecard had arrived that morning. The region had not met its performance goals, and as usual the regional vice president had scheduled an afternoon conference call with the nine district managers.

It had snowed the night before, and that led to the usual number of employee absences, late line-haul and aircraft arrivals, snowed-in trucks, and angry customer calls. All this only made worse the huge amount of preparation required to justify the previous month's performance, and with the snow, it was inevitable that there would be another conference call to explain *this* month's bad numbers *next* month. For district managers it was an endless cycle of long days, overworked staff, and ceaseless explanations about why the scorecard numbers looked bad.

After overseeing the late morning dispatch of 60 delivery trucks, the operations manager had locked himself in his office with the pile of last month's reports and worked through

*(Continued)*

**WHEN POOR PERFORMANCE IS ACTUALLY GOOD**
*(Continued)*

the day preparing a justification for his district's performance. It didn't help that the computer reports were generated by a different application than the paper reports and often failed to tie out. He called supervisors into his office, even placed a call to one at home, to create narratives for 16 missed pickups from the weeks in question. After that, he called other district managers to learn the groups' joint excuses. All of this took place in between the usual daily reporting requirements and an endless stream of telephone calls. Because this took the entire day, he had to cancel the weekly Thursday morning operations meeting, which would have set the staffing needs for the coming week.

The climactic outcome of all this was to analyze the previous month's performance during a two-hour conference call in which he spoke for approximately 15 minutes, answering specific questions on individual missed pickups, some over a month old, and explained why delivery in lower Manhattan was bad during the recent holiday. The remaining time was spent listening to the truly poorly performing managers getting beat up on any number of subjects, ranging from scorecard reports to their local shop steward parking in the visitor parking spots, topics often unrelated to issues that significantly impacted company or even district-level performance. However, because the vice president had them on the telephone, he wanted to bring the issues up and get them off his desk.

As he finished telling his story, an odd thought struck us: not only had this manager accomplished nothing that day because of *last* month's performance, but also, right then, during this dinner meeting, nothing was still getting accomplished because of it.

The vice president would have been surprised to discover that his conference call had accomplished nothing and had, in fact, set back the performance of his managers, if for no other reason than causing the cancellation of operations' meeting. There was not a single matter that was discussed or reported on that day that was not already known or would change future behavior.

The true change had occurred the previous month, after the holiday, when the manager's staff had set in place a solution. The conference call did little more than delay the day's work and frustrate the staff. It did nothing to ensure that these mistakes would not happen again.

The manager told us that he wasn't frustrated because he had to answer for the errors of his district; that was, after all, one aspect of his job. His true frustration came from knowing that next month would be the same. He would be answering for the bad numbers that would appear on his scorecard because of the snow last night. His district had actually performed fairly well during this very difficult situation. They had planned on extra drivers the night before because

*(Continued)*

---

**WHEN POOR PERFORMANCE IS ACTUALLY GOOD**
*(Continued)*

of the approaching front, supervisors had arrived early and had delayed the driver start time to save on overtime, routes had been redispatched, and problem equipment had been replaced. Still, regardless of these actions, delays had been inevitable and customers would be unhappy. Hours beyond the budget had been spent, overtime would still be high, and productivity would be low.

From the perspective of senior management, the manager and his staff had performed *poorly* because back in their offices they didn't know *why* until he explained it to them.

---

Employees who are actively involved in managing only one operation or process on a daily basis inherently believe that they understand why performance is what it is. For the most part, they are likely to be correct, but this inherent understanding usually does not make their jobs easier. Very often, they must deal with multiple systems, paper reports, and multiple departments to get the information they need to solve the problem they intimately understand. At lower levels of the organization, employees rarely stop to consider the larger business issues their managers are dealing with as they attempt to achieve strategic goals; lower-level employees focus on the transactional information that they use each day to do their jobs. It should be acknowledged that, in most organizations, lower-level employees are not even given the opportunity or the credibility to address organizational issues above their status. Management may listen but often reserves the right to be all-knowing.

For management, the problem becomes more difficult. Managers are responsible for multiple, interrelated areas or processes. They cannot clearly see what is happening within each of these the way they could when they were responsible for only one area or process. The more interrelated areas a manager is responsible for, the more difficult it is to determine the root cause of a problem. In most environments, management spends a significant amount of time figuring why things aren't going as planned, and then, when time has run out, managers resort to what worked in the past because it is the easiest way to get a quick, even if short-term, fix. Determining why something is actually wrong is often time-consuming and leads to the frustration experienced by the district manager in our story.

For senior management and executives, the performance puzzle becomes even more complicated. With limited time to manage diverse areas, the ability to see quickly where and why performance is off plan becomes even more critical.

Executives, managers, and employees all share this common need—the need to understand very quickly, *why* things they personally are responsible for are going wrong. For all employees, *why* is the bottom layer of the power grid and the performance portal. (See Figure 7.1.)

At the lowest level, the answer to *why* is fairly simple. For the pension fund, a customer case was delayed because some or all of

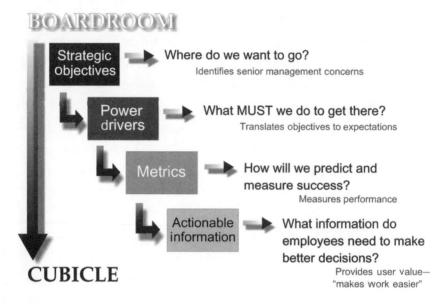

**Figure 7.1** Critical Performance Components

the paperwork required to process it was not turned in. The case processor needed to see quickly why it was delayed, which paperwork was missing. The missing paperwork ultimately caused delays in processing time. The supervisor of case processors was responsible for ensuring that all cases would be processed in a timely manner. He needed to know why this didn't happen. In simplest terms, he either had too many new cases to process (a large group of unexpected retirees), or didn't have enough employees to process them (due to absenteeism, vacation, holidays, or granted days off). He needed to know why so he could go do something about it.

For our logistics client, it was critical for operations to know beforehand whether a shipment would reach its destination by the commitment date, and if not, why. Shipments would be delayed for specific reasons: raw materials missing due to customer or vendor delays, warehouse pick/pack or loading delays, over the road shipping time requirements, or sales making a commitment that simply could not be met due to standard processing time requirements. If they knew why, they could do something to prevent failure.

Our client's district manager spent his time collecting reasons why things went wrong, why drivers missed pick-ups, why drivers were delayed getting out of the building, and why shipments were delivered late. His needs were actually the same as the regional manager's; they both needed to know why. The district manager simply couldn't distract his subordinates by having them gather the reasons for him as the regional manager could, so he wasted his own day doing it. Senior management rarely feels the pain of not understanding *why* as severely as lower-level managers do throughout the organization because senior managers typically have an army of assistants to gather this information for them whenever they need it—even if that army of employees has other things they are responsible for.

Searching for *why* prevents action. The power grid draws on the data within the organization to explain why things are the way they are—good performance or bad. With one click, it explains why the indicator is red, yellow, or green, freeing up managers to take action. Action is based upon factual information and truth, not inherent beliefs and biased opinions. If your organization is using a scorecard (a scorecard updated on a daily basis) to report on performance, then you have given management only half the picture. Management still needs to know why before it can actually do anything.

For executives, the answers, when broken down, can be simple, too. Why is profitability down? The answer can only be that revenue has dropped, expenses have increased, or both. Why has revenue dropped? Why have expenses increased? The metrics point directly to problem areas, and the string of *why*s paints a clear picture both for executives and for those directly responsible for the results. Action is taken and the impact of those actions is quickly seen.

For all of these levels, understanding why makes their jobs easier. By providing information that would otherwise have been difficult to get, the performance portal becomes a source of information and not another mandated management tool. This is a key to its success at overcoming traditional barriers to change.

*Why* is asked by nearly every manager in every organization every day. Every answer lies right there at their fingertips, yet it might as well be buried. For most of them it is—buried in cumbersome management reports and detailed transaction-oriented applications. What they struggle to understand, the grid provides; what drains organizational energy is, in fact, the very thing that powers the grid and energizes the organization.

# CHAPTER 8

# Powering the Grid

■ ■ ■

On Wednesday, July 24, 2002, at 3:00 P.M., 15 miners descended 249 feet into the Quecreek Number 1 Mine in Pennsylvania. Five hours later there was a break in a wall and 50 million gallons of water inundated the mine. The crew was working at different locations in the mine at the time and six miners were able to crawl onto a conveyer belt and move along it above most of the water. After crawling 2,500 feet, they managed to evacuate the flooding mine. Nine others were trapped. They moved to the highest point in their portion of the mine and waited.

Above ground, the company immediately threw all of its resources into a rescue effort. The cost might bankrupt the small company, but as the CEO said, "You don't send men into black holes then leave there to die. I know every man down there by his first name." During the early preparations for rescue there was no indication the nine men were still alive. However, early Thursday morning, contact was established by telephone. A pipe was then extended down to where the men were huddled and rescuers began pumping in warm air.

Volunteer miners from throughout the country traveled to Pennsylvania to help. Teams were organized and a plan was implemented. A rescue hole was cut almost at once and the company sent for a rescue capsule to descend through the hole. Below ground the cold water rose steadily. The men had no food or extra clothing. They clung to the pipe emitting warm air. Then they huddled together to preserve body temperature. It was a race between their stamina and the rising water.

For three days the Black Wolf Coal Company, its miners, and volunteers bored through the earth toward their nine men. Against all odds they reached the miners shortly after midnight Sunday morning. Food and warm drinks were sent down. The rescue capsule was in place and beginning at 1:00 A.M., one by one, the nine miners were pulled to the surface. It was an all but unprecedented rescue made possible by proper focus and execution.

■ ■ ■

The Pennsylvania miners caught in the mine collapse feared for their lives. Workers in companies about to experience a full rollout of the power grid can fear for their jobs. To avoid this, power must be properly applied to the grid.

Doing this starts when someone within the organization believes that the organization can be more than it is today. This person, a senior manager or a group of key managers, must then champion the power grid initiative. From there a select group of key individuals in the organization identifies the objectives, the power drivers, and the metrics. Many other managers and employees might be interviewed in order to determine the power drivers and their relationship to specific units within the organization, but up to this point in the process there is generally very little demand on their time. At this point, a large part of the organization does not understand *why* the power grid is being installed, and *why* it will make their jobs easier when so many other initiatives have only made it more difficult.

To overcome these obstacles, the most effective way to power the grid is to begin with a pilot program. This shows the organization, for the first time, what it will really be like to work in an environment where information is readily available and freely flowing; it shows how it works and the results that can be achieved. Perhaps most significantly, it is important to demonstrate how the power grid makes everyone's job easier.

Why launch the power grid as a pilot program? Purely because it is the most likely way to succeed. The organization as a whole may not understand its power and may believe it is just another management initiative. To overcome this, there needs to be immediate success. However, because the organization doesn't know what it's like to manage on the power grid, a pilot program provides a way for everyone to feel its power.

A pilot project is typically launched in one location, division, or department. Its manager should be not only someone who appreciates new ideas, but preferably someone who would also be technology friendly. This manager is a critical component to the overall success of the pilot project and must have, or report to someone with, the authority to make and enforce key decisions.

The initial goal of the pilot project is to overcome the two primary reasons that Enterprise Performance Management (EPM) initiatives fail within organizations. First, because EPM initiatives are unique to each organization, because the objectives, drivers, and metrics are specific to each organizational environment, the initial effort often becomes so complex that the organization can never get off the ground. Because the organization can't take these first few steps, as a whole it reverts to what it already knows, typically, the following: "We have too much going on to consider the initiative right now," "Profits were down last quarter and we have to focus on getting them back up first," or "We don't have the bandwidth for another change program." The methodology behind the power grid was specifically created to help the organization overcome these common stalling tactics. If you have read to this point and these excuses still hold water for your organization, then you have entirely missed the point.

Just as each person fears individual change, the organization fears it too. That is why the power grid takes a softer approach, and sets aside traditional change management theories while providing a structure to prevent the organization from getting lost during the process. It puts bumpers on the side of the road to keep the organization heading in the right direction. It prevents a reversion to what the organization has always done to achieve superior, sustainable performance—nothing.

The second reason that EPM initiatives fail is because users find nothing of value in it once the pilot is launched. You have built it but no one comes. Why? Because it doesn't make anyone's life within the organization easier. You have only created one more technology layer that muddies the water with cloudy data. You have not created information. That is why, during this entire initiative, it must start and remain strictly about addressing business needs, not implementing a new technology. If the initiative devolves into a technology implementation, any improvement in performance is unlikely and sustainable superior performance is nearly impossible. Technology is merely an enabler.

Again, the power grid methodology was created to overcome this second problem. The structure of this book follows the process an organization must go through. The initial chapters defined the process that will ensure that when you reach this point—launching of the pilot—users will find value in your creation. If the pilot had been launched in Chapter 1, you would almost definitely have failed in the end to create superior, sustainable performance across the organization.

By this point in the process (and in this book), the metrics have been defined. They are essentially math calculations performed on filtered data sets from one or more transactional applications. The actionable information that explains to users why performance is what it is has also been defined. In reality, this information is a combination of key data fields, also from specific transactional applications, often enhanced by the technology behind the grid. All this data comes from legacy systems that your organization is already using. In them lies data that has been accumulating for years but has not yet been leveraged.

For pilot purposes a vertical segment of the organization's metrics is selected. These are the metrics that apply to the pilot location, division, or department. Typically, they are metrics that would easily apply to other areas of the organization (such as processing time, which is influenced by many different locations, divisions, or departments), so that during full rollout the work done during the pilot is easily leveraged. Just as the pilot should seek to show value in no more than two or three months, full rollout should also show a quick return for each new area.

The next step is to examine legacy systems and all existing IT applications to determine that the data required for each metric is available to support the pilot. These legacy systems are already in place and generally hold over 75 percent of the data needed to calculate every metric. With creative thinking, those figures can reach 80 to 90 percent. Key data can also come from desktop applications, such as spreadsheets, because many organizations manage via Excel-mania and support processes and procedures with manager-controlled spreadsheets. The enabling technologies for the power grid can use that data as well as data in legacy systems.

We advise companies to work with data that already exists for the pilot launch. If there is a metric that the team thinks is important but the data to calculate it is not currently captured, just let it go. It is not necessary to get all the individual parts of the power grid perfectly aligned in the pilot. The pilot is a proof of concept.

A power grid pilot is like building a house. The blueprints are required before the house can actually be built because the owners won't have a proper sense of perspective until it is. They can't decide on details like room colors and furniture placement until they have it. The pilot gives this to them.

In the beginning, there is no standardized, strong, and effective process to ensure that data sets are accurate and consistent. When dealing with older IT applications, proper data controls are rarely in place to filter out differences from one program to the next. These differences can be as simple as the format for entering a date—some allow four digits, some just two. These issues need to be addressed so that data moving forward is reliable and consistent. Do not take the easy route and fix data outside of its natural legacy location; fix the problems that caused it or you will deal with those problems forever. It is not unusual for an IT system to reflect the way a company looked 20 years ago. For this reason, systems typically show something very different from the current organizational chart. The power grid will help the organization clean and improve data inconsistencies. Do not strive for perfection when launching the pilot; it will come with time. When the pension fund first turned on the grid and reviewed processing time, it was over 900 days per case. Why? Inconsistent data and flawed processes, policies, and procedures.

This too is an intentional aspect of the power grid. This approach allows the initiative to show quick value by improving processes and procedures immediately, tightening policies, and implementing additional controls. The power grid will essentially tell the organization where it is weak, so that process improvement initiatives can immediately focus on these areas. Process improvement initiatives, as a first step, typically conduct a series of process reviews in order to locate the areas of opportunity. It is only after all the potential areas have been reviewed that improvements are actually determined and implemented. The organization is spending a significant amount of time trying to figure out where the problems are before it can even do anything about them. With the power grid, this ratio is reversed. The process improvement initiative itself is more effective because management spends very little time determining where the problems are, and much more time fixing them. In addition, the power grid tells the organization which areas will have the biggest impact and, therefore, show the highest return. All of this creates a return and makes life easier within the organization.

One of the frequent surprises experienced with legacy data is the number of transactions that are simply lost. The pension fund found out that cases were still assigned to people who no longer worked within the organization. In some cases, employees were assigned to a special task in a different office for a year and their entire caseload was left at their desk while they were out of the country. Every organization's existing data will have problems of this type. The technology behind the grid is well equipped to handle this.

This technology comes in many packages under many names but generally they are called Enterprise, Business, or Corporate Performance Management (EPM/BPM/CPM) applications, and came from the arenas of business intelligence, analytical analysis, or budgeting and forecasting solutions. Many organizations already own one or more of them and use the power grid methodology to leverage what they have already invested in. It is the practical answer to achieve what they were promised when they purchased the software. Each application can have widely varying costs, features, and functionality, and, like any product, they are constantly being improved and expanded.

Part of the beauty of the power grid is that it can work with any of these various technologies. Certainly some are better equipped to handle the specific needs of each organization but, by and large, each can be utilized as the backbone to change the very nature of how the organization is managed and performs. The power grid becomes the user manual that business managers, not technology developers, will understand and can follow to achieve the results they are looking for.

Some IT managers and developers will understand that this is about technology addressing business needs and supporting them; it is not a software implementation. It is important that the power grid initiative remains in the hands of business managers, and is supported by IT—to the extent that they are willing.

In every power grid implementation, there will be some opposed to change. We have found that the group who most often opposes these performance initiatives is the IT department. From their perspective, the power grid would be providing much greater value to the organization than most of the current IT systems. This will inherently cause them to feel threatened. This approach and technology goes against most of what they have been taught and what they are familiar with. Since they are uncomfortable with the solution it is natural that they will try to derail the process. In this way they are resisting change, even though they don't realize that this is what they are doing. It is homeostasis at work.

Once the pilot is running, it will be a management-controlled application, managed by an administrator, not a developer. This puts the power in the hands of those who control the power drivers and the metrics, not the IT department. In most of today's business environments, IT has gained significant influence over line management, even to the extent that line management is often unwilling to stand up against them. This may be due to the promise of technology solving business problems, even though that promise is seldom realized.

It is also possible to find the finance department resistant to the power grid. For the past two decades, finance has been increasingly pushed into the role of owning information for most companies. The problem is that most finance people think in accounting terms. Their thinking is historic and confined to a spreadsheet. Even worse, their information and spreadsheets rarely focus on what drives performance in the company. They do not focus on the nonfinancial information that business leaders need in order to manage effectively, and *nonfinancial* information, the action-result relationship between operational performance and financial results, is at the heart of management within the power grid.

An organization's financial performance is a result of its ability to effectively and efficiently execute—operational performance drives financial results. This is the primary reason business needs must drive the initiative instead of finance or IT. This is not to say that a CFO or CIO cannot champion the power grid. They sometimes do, but it is a rare manager or executive who is willing to look outside his personal comfort zone for a solution (although, because information is power, these initiatives are often a good way to boost one's personal influence throughout the organization).

As the organization begins rolling out the power grid, the first thought of many managers is to use the power grid as an accountability tool. We urge companies not to turn the power grid into a stick. If that happens, employees quickly become turned off and work to manipulate and sabotage the system. The amazing thing about the power grid is that discussions about accountability never take center stage. What comes with the grid is visibility and transparency. Everyone's performance is reflected in simple, clearly stated terms. There is no hiding from the results or hidden agendas. The best way to prod employees toward greater performance is through individual competitiveness created by showcasing performance for all to see.

Once the pilot model is launched, managers and employees will quickly understand and experience the value it adds to them, even if they don't necessarily see the value to the organization as a whole. This value quickly takes center stage. Accountability and fear retreat to the background. Everyone is focusing on the grid, how it makes their life easier, and what it is doing for them.

Managers talk to employees and ask, "What would really help you? What is it you really need to see?" With such input, managers start to improve the power grid and the metrics are modified, added to, or replaced, and even more value is created. Soon those in the pilot program are receiving new information regarding their job and performance against objectives. Because they are seeing new things, they are soon asking for more information. Evolution takes hold. Excitement is generated and a company-wide buzz begins.

This is also the purpose of the pilot—to create that buzz. Employees within the pilot area will begin talking about this power grid and how they can see and do things so much easier now. This sets the stage for the much easier organization-wide implementation that will follow.

Once the pilot is up and running and the organization is comfortable with it, the next step is to expanding it throughout the organization. This is typically done by moving to adjacent departments that touch upon the areas already defined within the pilot. Often a significant amount of the work done on the pilot will also apply directly to these units. They may have slightly different nuances, or choose to see reports containing slightly different information, but the core of what they do, their power drivers, are typically closely related to one another.

Generally this expansion is easy to accomplish, even for those departments that have different power drivers, if only because they see its value and are eager for its application. It is also much easier to expand the initiative, building upon what you have already done, than it is to lay the first few building blocks of the foundation. However, as each department is added, they should still follow the general principles that applied as the pilot was launched. It is always important to ensure that they are confident in the data being used and, therefore, in the information it is providing. As each unit is added, the overall corporate performance portal starts to take on a life of its own. Before you know it, everyone is operating within the power grid and performance is multiplying.

The rollout process takes, on average, six months to a year, varying widely based upon organizational complexity. Generally, we would run a pilot for at least one month before rolling out the model throughout the organization, but it needs at least enough time to prove that the information contained in the portal is accurate. It should run long enough to know it will work and for people to have confidence in it. As it takes hold in each unit, the demand to implement it elsewhere begins to increase. Managers who aren't on the grid start asking for it. Their life is suddenly much easier and others can see that change. When the power grid is moving of its own volition, we find ourselves spending more and more time trying to control the natural growth. Once this happens, it is no longer about change; it is about other employees wanting their job to be that easy.

The result: power is multiplied. Like Quecreek, as more rescuers arrive, excitement builds, and this drives performance toward the all-important objective.

Desire trumps fear every time.

CHAPTER 9

# Managing
# on the Grid

...

**E**xecutives are used to chaos, uncertainty, and mismanagement. It can be frightening the first time everything goes smoothly. More than one CEO has related to us that the experience of suddenly standing alone wondering what to do was discomforting. There were no employees to discipline or fire. No customer complaints. No fires to put out. The end of chaos was, for many, an unsettling experience.

## THE CEO AS KING

One of our clients, the owner of a closely held company, was skilled in the role of CEO as king. He was clearly The Boss. If something was important to him, it was important to everyone. He made it clear that decisions of any significance were to be cleared through him. Although decisive, he also kept changing the rules and moving from one strategy to another. Everyone except the CEO experienced confusion and a lack of continuity. Like many companies governed this way, financial performance was weak and inconsistent.

After several years of operating with mediocre results, the CEO asked us to help him accomplish two objectives:

■ Improve profits.
■ Improve his management team.

When we completed our assessment, a clearer picture emerged. This was a highly conflicted man. He wanted to change, but could not live with the consequences.

We worked with the CEO to develop power drivers and metrics for his objectives. We stressed focusing on the company's future. We then discussed his reluctance to loosen his grip on decisions. We concluded by building a vision for him in which his managers were more than firefighters or slaves, there to do his bidding.

Every manager was excited about the new objectives. They expressed eagerness to change what they were doing. Each was sure that moving toward a new management culture would do wonders for the company.

One of the steps in the process was a management summit. There we discussed the CEO's objectives and other power grid–related issues. As the summit proceeded, it became clear that there was a strong undercurrent of doubt that what we were talking about could be achieved. Everyone was saying the right things, but no one seemed to really believe that it was possible.

With some coaxing, the CEO finally verbalized his key issue: "If we make these changes and give managers the authority and responsibility to make all these decisions, what am I going to do?" It became crystal clear to him that the biggest change was his to make. It was also apparent that if he was not willing to loosen his grip, none of what he envisioned would happen.

Just about every manager at the summit knew that the CEO's concern would surface. They felt it too. They were used to running into his office with a problem and waiting for him to give them the solution. If he changed, what were they going to do?

We showed the group that with the power grid everyone

*(Continued)*

143

---

**THE CEO AS KING** *(Continued)*

would have more time to drive results. The CEO would have the time to meet with customers, think about the future direction of the company, keep a closer watch on the market, and monitor the results of what was really happening in his company. He would remain the captain of the ship, but with a crew devoted to accomplishing his mission.

It was not an easy transition, but they all made it. Today, the company is successful and the management team is highly effective.

---

Fear of success is a powerful force, more powerful than most executives imagine. Our client, the CEO king, was afraid of ending the chaos. All roads led to him. He made every decision of any importance within his company. He was needed. He envisioned himself as indispensable. That was pretty heady stuff.

When the power grid was set in place, all this CEO needed to do was establish a direction for his company and, as we jokingly advised, take the rest of the year off. What CEOs and executives actually do is begin to devote their time and talent to the company's strategic objectives, customer relations, and management development. The freedom to focus energy in those critical areas has as much to do with creating an outstanding organization as anything else. Managers become more effective because they are riveted to the things that matter. Short- and long-term performances are improved because senior managers are concentrating on longer-term strategic objectives.

With long-term metrics and drivers, the CEO and senior managers quickly discover what managing really means. Give the CEO an indicator that shows him market trends for the next month, quarter, and year and see if he really comes up with nothing to do that day.

This is what the Performance Power Grid creates within organizations. Not instantly, not the moment the pilot is launched, but with increasing speed and energy from the moment the grid initiative begins focusing energy and effort.

Keep in mind that initially not everyone will agree on the objectives, power drivers, and metrics in the performance portals. Some managers will want to include other measures for any number of reasons. However, the initial analytical decision on the objective/power driver/metric relationship creates an initial agreement on how performance will be viewed. When this first happens, *everyone has a common language.* From that point on, managers and supervisors begin talking about the same things around the water cooler. In a diverse company, with semi-autonomous divisions, this can often be the only way to get everyone on the same page. That is a powerful force that drives organizational performance at all levels and allows the organization to see things they never saw before, and see themselves in a completely new light.

As the organization begins to learn things about itself that it never knew before, as it sets aside cultural bias and beliefs, it begins to understand that how it saw things in the beginning of the power-grid initiative might not have been exactly right.

This is one of the reasons why having precisely correct metrics at first is not necessary. Everyone being on the same page allows the correct metrics to evolve. Metrics that are meaningless will go away. Those that are missing, but are needed, will be added. Because managers are seeing the same overall picture through the metrics, a consensus emerges. In this way the power grid removes personalities from the battle. Turf fights largely vanish. Scapegoating is no longer an acceptable management style.

Even though it is not discussed very often, the power grid really is about accountability. However, it isn't about blame. Competent managers want to perform well and will not mind being held accountable. For that reason, top managers, the company's real producers, will shine in this new environment.

What was chaos and confusion is now clear. The fog of business is lifted. Instead of repeating the same actions, managers now adjust their performance to fit what is actually happening. Instead of dwelling on the past, they see the future. They can now do something about bad trends. Personalities, office politics, the ability to smooth-talk or evade responsibility are all diminished. The truly effective managers emerge; no one can hide behind a ready smile or the latest Madison Avenue fashion statement.

We've emphasized that the system need not be perfect at each step in order for it to work. The point is to get the process started. For many, the power grid doesn't make real sense until it is turned on. They can't visualize a different future. We have seen it again and again. Managers who engaged the power grid with reservations soon say, "This is great, but if you could make it do _____, it would be perfect." That is when we know they get it.

During the rollout, there will be meetings with every unit of the company to explain the principles of the power grid. These meetings serve a number of purposes. One of the most important is to alleviate fear. Too often employees picture any new management tool only as a means for greater accountability, with no benefit. This is one reason why a pilot is so important. Employees need to see for themselves or hear from co-workers the value that comes from the power grid.

We cannot overemphasize the importance of addressing the fear of accountability. Acknowledge it head on. One company lightheartedly told employees that if supervisors used the power grid as an accountability tool, at least it would be an honest one. Job responsibilities and performance criteria were clear. The only person who should fear the power grid, they said, was someone who really didn't want to work anyway.

In our experience, most employees are competent and want to do well. Given the right tools, they can do even better. Most people do not fear reasonable accountability; they fear being held accountable for the unknown. What they want is clearly defined roles and responsibilities, and ironically, what they want is exactly what they need.

The power grid and the performance portal create a cultural shift in how a company works and is managed. One of the most dramatic changes is how management meetings are conducted. When utilizing the power grid, managers come to a meeting and start with where they are today. If someone should have taken care of something since the last meeting, the problem will still exist; it will be part of today. Questions don't revolve around "What happened?" Instead they focus on, "How are you taking care of this? What do you need to ensure we don't fail here?" Or they are specific and tied directly to issues that affect management: "What is the plan to collect the outstanding debts in the next ten days?" These questions fundamentally change the dynamics of management.

Everyone knows the key metrics and how they are performing against the plan. Attention will begin to focus on the yellow lights—those areas where action can still affect the future. The power grid eliminates meetings where everyone arrives with the 400-page report and a list of excuses. What's the point of excuses when the indicators tell the whole story? Some CEOs have gone so far as to project their own portal on the wall and use it as the basis for the meeting.

It doesn't take long before employees and managers fully grasp the power and common language of the grid. They find it easier to talk to employees about objectives and they don't have to waste time trying to get employees to understand strategy.

The grid's common language gives managers time to work on a solution before the CEO even asks the question. In most cases the manager's indicator goes yellow *before* the boss's. When the portals become the foundation of discussions, answers are usually in place before the meeting.

Actually, those meetings are no longer key moments for the organization; performance is part of its very nature. When the CEO in our story visited his performance portal and discovered that collections were coming as projected, he realized that something important was taking place. The organization was moving forward without his direct intervention. This realization can be unsettling, but it is also liberating.

Once a CEO or management team begins managing on the power grid, there comes a point when they move from dealing with the tactical to considering the strategic. Suddenly, and perhaps for the first time in years, the CEO has an opportunity to ask critical, business-related questions: "What are competitors doing? Where's the market? Where are we in it? What unexploited opportunities are there?" Take those same thoughts throughout the organization and imagine the power that could create.

To reach this point is an evolutionary process. Managing on the power grid ensures that that unsettling but liberating day will come, and it will arrive sooner than most CEOs think. Imagine things in your own organization being this different next quarter.

Despite the central role of the CEO, the power grid and the performance portals should not be controlled or managed by one specific person. The grid will have an administrator to handle day-to-day details but within each unit, managers are in charge of their own metrics. The indicators themselves are changed only after consulting with senior managers, whose job is to ensure that they remain linked to the power drivers, but even that conversation is intentional and important. What better way to improve future performance than having managers and their bosses sitting down to discuss the impact their unit is having on overall success?

It takes courage for a management group to manage on the power grid. It requires a new way of thinking, a new approach to problems, and a willingness to surrender the illusion of control. If courage slackens and trust in the motivating power of the grid weakens, the CEO can become the single greatest obstacle to managing on the grid. Executives must have the discipline to abide by its concepts. Part of the process of implementing the grid is agreeing that this is how the organization is going to manage itself and that management is going to let employees do the jobs they were hired to do.

Some senior managers want to roll out the power grid only to the management group. We discourage that. The power grid should be applied to all levels of an organization, at least down to the lowest management level. The power grid is an *organizational* performance tool applied to each layer of the organization. Action takes place in cubicles and on shop floors more often than in expensively furnished boardrooms and corner offices. That is where the real return is.

This is as it should be and how the modern-day management model was intentionally created to operate. Small businesses, to a large extent, still operate this way. Often, the corner office is only a few doors away from the shop floor. The bigger the business, the further that walk to talk to employees becomes, until eventually, the distance is too great to cross. The Performance Power Grid bridges that modern-day gap.

CHAPTER 10

# Throwing the Switch

...

**M**odern-day businesses are often managed like the *RMS Titanic*. They are designed for business as usual; they pay little attention to the surrounding environment. Employees become passengers who cannot alter the course of their organization even if they hear the dreaded cry, "Iceberg dead ahead." It is only after feeling the impact that a response occurs. With a deep hole and badly damaged, the organization's own inertia forces it to remain on a doomed course, driving more and more water into its hull. Some sink; some limp into port long overdue.

Getting to New York wasn't the primary goal of the *Titanic*; getting the passengers and crew safely across the ocean was. The captain paid for this mistake with his life; he took a lot of people and his entire organization with him. Properly managed, the

*Titanic* would have completed its voyage in safety. The captain of that ship, Captain Smith, would have lived to enjoy his place in history.

This misinterpretation of what is important is the primary reason for constant mediocrity. Interpretation itself is a problem. Most managers simply don't understand what drives the success of their company. No one ever took the time to develop power drivers or had a clear method to connect an individual's work with company objectives. There was never a practical solution with which to do this or with which to see the future. These omissions force every manager to constantly assess and reassess their purpose and priorities. They fill every manager's day with clutter and noise, constantly distracting them from focusing on improvements that would actually lead them out of this hazy confusion.

The power grid ends all that, once and for all. It paints a clear picture of the organization and what is driving it. It tells every manager where they stand and gives each one simple roadside directions that are tailored to explain where each manager is going and how to get there. It is the clarity of this picture and the clear instructions that finally solves the performance puzzle.

A great deal of the Performance Power Grid's power comes from the fact that a CEO doesn't have to adopt a different management model. Managers don't really have to change how they are managing; employees aren't required to buy into something they neither understand nor believe in. The key is to change what they are focused upon. Focus on those things that truly drive your success, and success will follow.

The power grid is not a replacement for performance improvement models. A company can continue to use the Balanced Scorecard, Six Sigma, or any other model with which it has had success. The power grid becomes the engine that takes performance to the next level. It is the framework that makes everything the organization does stand up to the test of time and market leadership.

We have seen the transformation in other companies. We witness it every day in our own. Since implementing the power grid, we have become the company in our industry against which many others measure their performance. We've seen it work. We have created it and then tested it in diverse environments, refining it along the way. We have seen that the power grid methodology applies everywhere, regardless of the industry, the current status of the company, or the challenges a company is facing.

Why? Because at its core the power grid is about people. People take action. They may succeed or fail in their intent, but they are the very foundation of business. They will not change, not simply because they are asked to, and certainly not overnight. People work in both boardrooms and cubicles.

People require something to change them, and something to prevent a reversion back to old habits. The power grid provides both of these. Traditional change management methods have not changed in decades. If the approach toward change itself cannot change in the face of failure, then as a methodology it will never help organizations achieve success.

Implementing the Performance Power Grid was intentionally

designed not to be disruptive. As business managers ourselves we understand that the wheel of business does not stop turning, and will not stop while the grid is implemented. Although its effects are profound, the grid does not require an enormous investment of time or energy to create. It builds upon what the organization already has in place, its present staff and IT system, things they are already familiar with. The Performance Power Grid approach is so adaptable that it easily applies to enterprise risk management, risk-based auditing, real-time compliance, the requirements of the Sarbanes-Oxley Act, and corporate governance.

Some readers are undoubtedly thinking that it can't be this simple. However, simplicity is behind some of the great inventions of the business world. The paperclip is just a piece of wire. The Post-It note is just glue and paper. Both are simple; both are revolutionary business tools.

So many of the concepts managers try to implement are based on complex models. It seems to us that these concepts have made business more complicated than it really needs to be. At the end of the day, a company has a product or service it is trying to sell, one it wants to produce at the lowest possible cost, from which it hopes to make a reasonable profit. It is as simple as that. Companies must focus upon those basic components of their success.

Many CEOs and managers understand the logic of the power grid and see its potential, but they wait to do anything. They themselves cannot overcome their own fear of change despite the obviousness of its need. It is, after all, easier to tell someone else to change than to change oneself. They fail to see that they too are genetically controlled by homeostasis.

## Throwing the Switch

It takes a rare leader to break from this mold. Most require a crisis, an external trigger. In business, that trigger is usually something as big as hitting an iceberg. This book itself cannot change you and so we can only offer a bit more logic: it is easier to start now, while you are walking on that familiar treadmill, than when you are struggling to prevent yourself from drowning in icy water.

APPENDIX

# Real-Time Compliance

■ ■ ■

If you've been in logistics for any length of time, you can see everything you need to know about the health of a company in its warehouse. However, it's something you learn to keep your mouth shut about. People really don't want to know the truth about their organization as presented by the dirt and grime of this environment. They avoid the warehouse because it stares them in the face and presents things in a way that can't be avoided if you turn the lights up. They'd rather see it through their reports, on clean white paper.

In a warehouse with this much grime on its inventory, after only two days, the secrets couldn't wait to get out. In fact, they were hardly secrets. In the warehouse, organizational secrets are more like in-house jokes. If you're a good logistician you know how to yuck it up with the hourly employees and find out everything you need to know.

It was funny, though, watching an internal auditor, who five minutes ago admitted she couldn't figure out how they could store chemicals in musical instruments, search for specific inventory lots. She climbed over skids, squeezed in between pallets, and didn't even mind getting dirty. It took over an hour to find an inventory lot that hadn't moved in over ten years.

I enjoyed her antics; I knew they would end soon. Early that day, the dirt had told me the big secret. Almost half of this forty-million-dollar inventory hadn't moved in almost ten years.

No one laughed at the exit meeting when the external audit team reported that the inventory value reported in the financial statements hadn't accurately taken into account excess and obsolete inventory, and that the actual value was only half of the forty million. This was a material problem.

I did listen to how expensive it was to make chemicals as complex as they were manufacturing, and even to how expensive it was to dispose of this hazardous material they had created. I understood that, someday, there might be someone who needed this exact chemical they had been storing. I knew this plant only broke even; it made sense that they didn't waste their slim profits on disposal fees. I knew inventory value has always been a slightly gray area, so I nodded agreement with all of their excuses.

I also knew that at almost that exact same time in northern New Jersey, a CEO was picking up his four-year-old daughter from preschool. I had met her at his office about two months ago. There is no way he gave even a moment's thought to his inventory value as he fixed the new butterfly hair clip she was so proud to wear. If he wanted to be able to fix that same clip in her hair six months from now, he needed to know about this problem he'd never heard of before. It was a problem he hadn't created. However, his shareholders needed to know about it tomorrow or he could find himself in prison just a few months from now. The rules had changed—now it was personal.

■ ■ ■

Enron, WorldCom, and HealthSouth have become household names for the worst of reasons. The flagrant violations of public trust perpetrated by the managers of these companies dominated the nightly news for more than a year. Looting of these companies occurred on such a scale that it was as if pirates were controlling business. The accounting profession was rocked to its very core by the scandals. Millions of investors lost billions of dollars in retirement and investment savings.

In order to stop such abuses, Congress passed the Sarbanes-Oxley Act of 2002 (SOX). It required public companies to implement a robust internal control and financial reporting structure. It mandated that audit committees become much more active in their oversight role. Managers and the firm conducting the yearly external audits were not to go unnoticed. The Act required that the CEO and CFO certify to the Securities and Exchange Commission (SEC) that everything was disclosed that should be disclosed and that the company's system of internal control and financial reporting was in place and operating effectively.

Sarbanes-Oxley also subjected the CEO, CFO, or both, to severe penalties if they knowingly or willfully signed the certification with inaccurate statements. However, the Act went even further. It

163

stated that *regardless* of the CEO's or CFO's personal knowledge of any misconduct or misstatement, they were still subject to both monetary and criminal penalties. If it achieved nothing else, Sarbanes-Oxley took the age-old excuse, "I didn't know," out of play.

Under SOX, the external auditing firm must also provide a separate certification that the financial reports signed by the CEO and CFO were accurate. The external auditors must also issue a document stating their opinion about the internal controls of the organization.

Both of these added requirements, and indeed the entire act, were attempts to give shareholders greater security and confidence in American business. In the old days, managers were trusted to do the right thing. Now the market knew better.

Sarbanes-Oxley has forever changed the landscape of corporate financial reporting and a manager's responsibility. Ensuring that the assets of the company are safeguarded is now management's primary fiscal responsibility. Good corporate governance has always made sound business sense. Now it is management's responsibility to conduct its business in an ethical manner. Managers must ensure that all relevant factors—information that an investor or interested third party needs to know—are disclosed in the company financial statements. If a material event occurs, managers have just two days to publicly disclose it. If they do not, they run the risk of a full investigation, adverse publicity, and the penalties that may follow.

Two days. How quickly do two days pass in your business environment? How many fires take flame? How many management meetings are held to extinguish them? How quickly could your executive management team determine what happened, who was to blame, and what will be done about it? Could they also evaluate legal exposure, what *must* be reported, who might be liable, and then write and publish a suitable report and issue it to shareholders—all in two days?

Consider this scenario. On a Monday morning someone in your company's finance department determines that your inventory value has been falsely inflated. It seems local managers have not been properly identifying and accounting for excess and obsolete inventory each year. As a significant asset in most companies, inventory value has an important impact on company value. By the close of business on Tuesday, you must have publicly notified all shareholders of this discrepancy. What value will your company have when the market opens on Wednesday? By close of business on Wednesday an investigation will probably have begun.

The logic behind SOX is so straightforward, you wonder why it took scandals of such enormous magnitude to change the system. Clearly, something profound had gone wrong in corporate America. Greed created corruption that led some top managers to believe their own welfare was their first responsibility.

With constant earnings pressure on public-company management teams, it became easier to make decisions that met Wall Street and investor expectations. Like all such decisions, the more often they occurred, the easier and more egregious they became. Incentive bonus and stock option plans, like carrots in front of hungry mules, helped skew managers' judgment. Enormous wealth became more important than doing the right thing.

A high percentage of public company CEOs have their personal compensation directly linked to the profitability of their organization. For many, it is a significant portion of their income.

These same CEOs influence the reports that show company profitability. It is then left to the board of directors to oversee the CEO's performance and the health of the company. The board is at an unfair disadvantage because they never see reality through any lens but the CEO's.

Many CFOs also have their personal compensation tied directly to their company's financial performance. Most of them have unlimited access to the system that generates these reports. Even operational managers typically have unlimited access to the transactional systems of their company. Despite internal controls put in place by the audit group, these managers *could* modify the numbers or processes that reflect their performance. Their compensation is typically tied to company performance as well.

The old reporting structure was originally created to give assurance that what happened was published. However, this structure produced a false sense of security. Managers had some control over their compensation as well as the information going to those who were keeping an eye on them. How can a board of directors oversee a CEO when the only information to which they are privy is the information the CEO provides? They can't. The CEO knows the organization far better than they do. And so it goes down the line. Companies were performing three-way checks on accounting transactions for each penny they spent, but no such checks existed for reporting financial performance. Sarbanes-Oxley added a new wrinkle by making each management layer personally liable.

Every company in America has experienced change because of Sarbanes-Oxley. The impact is not limited to public companies. No one serving on the board of any company wants to be embarrassed or drawn into an enforcement action. For that reason, the actual effect of Sarbanes-Oxley may be even greater than legislators imagined.

Initially, though, two types of nonpublic organizations were most affected. One was the large not-for-profit organization that receives public funds through government grants, private donations, and endowments. These organizations usually have fairly active boards comprised of influential people who are politicians or executives in other companies. No board member is going to want to be on the board of the Enron of not-for-profits. These people are not going to tolerate public humiliation for a major fraud or corporate governance issue if they can avoid it. Such boards are now requesting that their organizations comply with Sarbanes-Oxley–like initiatives. Those initiatives include directing the CEO and CFO to sign certifications just like their public-company counterparts.

Large, privately owned companies are also affected. When they seek nonpublic financing from banks, venture capitalists, or private placements, they are discovering that these entities require Sarbanes-Oxley–like corporate governance. Because of this, the boards of such companies will be requiring auditors to certify the internal control framework just as they do in public companies.

For these and other sound reasons, all companies using other people's money should, or will soon have to, embrace these changes. The consequences for *not* knowing and *not* doing are just too high.

A part of the problem is, of course, that there is too much to know. Offices can be in different cities, states, and nations. Databases and IT systems employed by an organization are often not standardized or interconnected.

Part of the solution comes from those streams of data that have been generating reams of paper for years. These systems retain an enormous amount of information. Real-time compliance, a natural extension of the power grid framework, has the ability to pull in and link data from multiple disparate sources. It can, in effect, provide the three-way check that the organization now needs.

In a world where business moves at the speed of light, decision making is often decentralized. Organizations are spreading out in a global economy. There are more data sets than ever. These data sets offer a significant advantage. They provide an impersonal snapshot of company performance and the actions of its employees. Properly processed and tabulated, *data does not lie*.

IT supports the auditing, certifying, testing, and reporting needs of a company and puts that information into standard reporting formats. Quite often, though, IT data sets do not help managers understand or evaluate the overall performance or compliance effort of their companies, but the data does serve as an important source for internal auditors.

The power grid methodology, when applied to corporate governance and SOX compliance, provides management with insight into the inner-workings of its business environment. For the first time, real-time compliance is possible—compliance that shows where the organization stands at the current time. It shows the results of business decisions as they are being made, how they impact the future, and how key internal controls are operating throughout the company. Real-time compliance compares operations to financial results. It reveals trends and anomalies before it is too late to do something about them. In short, real-time compliance validates the financial statement for the executive.

## Appendix: Real-Time Compliance

With real-time compliance, a company should know well before the end of the period that it is going to miss its earning projections. The market and shareholders are more forgiving when they learn about problems early, but beyond that, foreknowledge allows time for something to be done about potential missed projections.

Consider again our client with headquarters in southern Florida. It sold its products predominantly through book fairs to students and their parents. Most fairs took place in the fall when excitement over the new school year was high. One year, southern Florida and the surrounding region was devastated by three successive hurricanes. Over 60 schools were destroyed. Numerous others in surrounding states were damaged.

The company sales department contacted schools and PTA administrators to verify each upcoming event. They cancelled those that could no longer be held. Local operations personnel spent their time cleaning up and inventorying a warehouse that was partially flooded. Local managers were bogged down with numerous details, not the least of which included determining if all company employees were alive, safe, and still had places to live. Understandably, absenteeism was at an all time high.

Behind the scenes, the power grid painted a picture of the company's future that didn't look good. There was no way the organization would achieve its fourth quarter and year-end revenue goals. The company was going to fall significantly short. The only upside was that managers saw this coming while they still had time to respond.

This enabled management to take a few simple actions. In order to increase revenue, they notified regional sales managers and division heads in unaffected states and overseas. They urged them to schedule additional school events in their locale. In order to make it easier for their sales force to accomplish this, the company allowed sales managers and division heads to offer a 10 percent discount to customers scheduling new events. They held a conference call and had their operations managers transfer inventory for high-demand products out of Florida to their other warehouses. This action increased revenue. They also requested that the Florida operations cut all overtime, thereby further reducing costs.

They took these actions in the real world using conference calls, e-mails, and memos. If that was all they had done, they might not have achieved their goals. Without the power grid, the company would have been at the mercy of each individual manager to change his or her behavior in ways that benefited the organization, but the increased stress within the organization made behavior change less likely. This is the dilemma faced by most companies not managing on the power grid.

However, because our client was on the grid, managers were able to follow through and ensure that employees changed their behavior. They updated the grid to reflect these changes and tracked these new key metrics. They knew, on a daily basis, if new events were added. They also knew if inventory was moving and overtime was really being reduced. Each manager, through a performance portal, saw his or her performance in these key areas. They constantly knew whether they were doing what senior management needed done to avert a crisis.

This is not simply real-time compliance. This is managing more effectively.

# Appendix: Real-Time Compliance

How does the chief executive know for certain that his financial statements are an accurate reflection of what is really going on in his organization? Actually, he doesn't.

Executives receive information reported to them by lower-level employees. Given the complexity of most organizations, senior managers cannot possibly know that the information reported is accurately reflected in day-to-day reality. Not all business mistakes are due to fraudulent activity, but, given the new standards created by Sarbanes-Oxley, it really doesn't matter. How can the CEO avoid this dilemma and the personal risk it creates?

Traditional methods of ensuring fiscal responsibility—monthly financial analysis and internal audits—reflect the past and do not give managers enough time to see if things are going wrong. Given the risk that managers face today, quarterly or yearly checks just are not good enough.

The best real-time window into the inner workings of an organization is the power grid coupled with its expansion into corporate governance. These tools give senior managers the best possible early warning system. With the grid, they can deal with issues before they become tomorrow's problems or tomorrow's front-page news.

# Afterword

Technology is in a constant state of flux. It is continuously growing in a life cycle that takes it from its birth as a niche solution, where it can be implemented and used only by highly technical professionals, to adulthood as a stable solution that may still require highly technical professionals to implement it, but is widely usable once implemented by the average business person. The technology that enables the Performance Power Grid, typically called Enterprise or Business Performance Management (EPM/BPM) applications or simply performance management (PM) applications (not to be confused with applications that service the human resources needs of organizations), has rapidly grown toward maturity as this book has been written and published.

What was by and large an unwieldy group of adolescents boasting of their as-yet unrealized full potential just six years ago is now a fully realized, user-friendly group of EPM applications that not only can be used by the average business person, but can also be *administered* by an average business person. Although this has traditional information technology managers rallying to the defense of older methods and taking up arms in opposition to this technology-for-the-masses movement, the appeal of this approach, and its potential, continues to grow unchecked.

Many organizations have already purchased these applications, or have been upgraded to them by mergers, acquisitions, and technology providers who realize we are now on the verge of a fundamental shift in the way organizations are managed and who did not want to lose their client base to this new market. As we have highlighted in case studies throughout this book some of those early adopters saw great success. However, many of the organizations that invested in this technology while undertaking performance initiatives (often buying several different, very expensive, applications) failed to get the return on investment and boost in performance they expected. At the initiative level this widespread failure typically occurred for common reasons.

Performance, or what drives superior performance, for each organization is different. Management cannot attend a conference and simply walk away with a roadmap that will take their organization from where it is today, to the utopia of data flow and information sharing that EPM as a methodology offers. Most often they walk away feeling that EPM offers the solution, but the future it presents and the changes it requires are so foreign to them and their organization that they are at a loss about where to start.

Because what drives the performance of each organization is unique, the final solution is therefore unique, and each organization cannot simply copy the answers from the organization taking the test at the desk next to them. Knowing there is an answer but not knowing how to realize it, they follow the modern business trend of throwing more technology at the problem.

This causes the initiative to fail because creating the power grid for an organization isn't about the technology; it is about people and what drives *them*—the way they manage and the way they work. This type of technology enables them to manage and work more effectively. In essence, it is what makes managing in this newer, more effective way, stick, and, therefore, it can't be overlooked as an important part of the overall solution. (However, there have been some organizations that have had surprisingly great success without using any technology but using just the approach itself.)

The EPM technology in this market space is in the midst of a Cambrian Explosion. And as with any market going through this stage in its life cycle, it is best that the buyer beware. Enterprise performance management and its related technology is one of the biggest modern-day management trends, and as such there are a lot of technology providers that want a piece of this large pie. Some of their applications were specifically designed for this type of application; some just got a new paint job, a vacuumed interior, and a new name that references performance as often as possible in its sales literature.

When we evaluate applications to decide if they meet the needs of the power grid (and we are approached with persistent regularity to do so) or that they meet the needs of one of our clients who is looking to enable a performance management initiative, we follow two criteria.

First, does the core functionality of the application represent the best-of-breed technology in the space it chooses to brand itself in (understanding that there may be more than one best or that there may be one at each significant price break)? This allows us to then decide which of these best-of-breed applications most meets the needs of each specific client straight out of the box—considering that the focus of each client initiative is different (financial, budgeting, analytics, operations, human resources, real-time compliance, or any combination of these).

Almost every technology will claim that it can meet virtually any client's needs. To be honest, almost any of them *could*. In truth you could create the basic technology behind the power grid with technology found in almost every business today, so any established technology of the day *could* be modified to do the job. However, just because it *could* doesn't mean it *should*. Modifications are expensive and turn your application into a can of worms waiting to pop open, requiring much greater effort and resources to maintain, upgrade, and grow throughout the organization. To avoid this problem, follow the process defined in this book. Understand your needs first, and then use what you have or find the right technology that was designed to best meet those needs.

The second criterion speaks more directly to the characteristics of the current Cambrian Explosion. Although EPM is sometimes considered an emerging market, it would be more appropriate to define it as a *created market*.

Enterprise Performance Management as a theory has grown from the combination of various management methodologies and technological approaches. Management by metrics, business intelligence, active analytics, executive information systems, dashboards, and even knowledge management were all separate niches, each with its own group of technology providers seeking to corner each of those markets. The biggest technology providers in these spaces saw the opportunity to bring them together (saw the opportunity to sell more products), and this new market was loosely labeled business performance management. (Although it is largely semantics, the difference between a BPM/CPM initiative and

EPM initiative is that BPM or CPM initiatives are typically applied in niche areas within an organization, whereas EPM initiatives often start in a niche area with the intent of becoming an enterprise-wide initiative and are implemented following a formal methodology, such as the power grid.) This early stage in the EPM life cycle was typical to that early stage in almost all technology life cycles, and was defined by highly technical implementations that required significant development and little practical, widespread usage. Given this layman's overview of the market, it is easy to see that many of those early implementations, driven purely by technology, would not return the value that the organization sought.

However, the sheer common sense solution that the theory provided caught on. It just makes too much sense. Once it began to gain traction, other application providers (some of whose products didn't really fit the market), in addition to new start-up companies, entered the market. Over time, the market has, as it always does, boiled the group of products and providers down to only those that truly provide value.

The new applications that continue to enter the market serve an important function; they constantly bring the technology to higher levels of both form and function. With good organizations behind them, they can offer businesses even greater flexibility, often at a lower overall cost, but it takes time to determine if these technologies can actually live up to their promises (despite what some research companies are paid to say and write about them). Therefore, given the state of the market, with its pluses and minuses, it is important to evaluate organizations in terms of their likelihood of still being in business even just one year from now.

# Afterword

To enable the power grid, we chose to partner with organizations that provided products with strong core functionality and that are following a stable financial model. We have learned over time that both criteria are equally important. Perhaps this is because, when the Performance Power Grid as a methodology was first created, we, as its creators, didn't know enough to put each technology into a separate bucket and allow each piece to solve only the problem it was originally created to address.

We started with the business problems we were trying to solve within our own organization, throughout our diverse careers, and within our client organizations, and then took the best piece of each technology and brought them together to create a practical solution. Many years and many more clients later, we have fully realized that technology was never the answer; it simply enabled the solution.

Technologies powered the alarm clock that woke you up this morning and the lights that allowed you to brush your teeth and get dressed, and enabled you to drive to work, do your job, prepare your dinner, call your family, and even purchase this book. However, the technology didn't *do any of those things—you did*, people did. People live, love, work, and produce. You read this book. You have the power to go out there and change things.

# Acknowledgments

**M**any people had a hand in making this book a reality, but without the support and unique talent of Ron Watkins, Celia Rocks, and Matt Holt it never would have happened.

David F. Giannetto:

By the time you finally sit down, at the very end of the writing process, to write an acknowledgment, you realize that for you, the author, the pages are full of so much more than just the words. The words pale in comparison to the conversations, the support, the celebrations, the hellos and goodbyes, and even the tears that you shared with those who were in your life throughout the process.

My family supported me in this as they have throughout my entire life; I give thanks each day that we are all so close. I would especially like to thank my father for having the courage and persistence to stay true to the vision that he believes in, and to live a life that he loves, and one of which I am deeply proud. Many people love what they do, but he does what he loves—every day. That is perhaps the greatest accomplishment in life and I hope that I can follow his example.

Ronald Pfeiffer has provided continuous support and belief in my abilities for nearly all my life. He is a truly great friend and an

## Acknowledgments

amazingly original graphic artist who put a significant amount of time and energy into this project.

Over the years I have been guided by great mentors and good friends, namely, Dale Carpenter, who first showed me what leadership and remaining true to your word is all about. Much of what I learned from him is contained in this book, including the responsibility of management to enable, protect, and promote their most talented employees.

Accomplishing so much in the Enterprise Performance Management space would not have been possible without the support and friendship of Carmela Owens—you deserve my thanks, and much more credit. Thanks and credit, also, to the support of all the clients, partners, and close relationships I have built with those who share my interest and passion for this theory.

My special thanks to Ron Watkins (an internationally respected author of 5 books) for teaching me how to write for the long haul, and to Celia Rocks for being very good at her job, as well as tough but honest.

I owe Anthony Zecca my thanks for giving me the time and support I needed to grow this tiny nugget of an idea we had over five years ago into the market-proven methodology it has become today.

Anthony Zecca:

This book is the result of many years of experience and interaction with so many clients and executives from whom I have learned so much. I wish to express thanks to my many partners at J. H. Cohn LLP, particularly Tom Marino, my friend and managing partner, for his support in this effort and my partners in the

## Acknowledgments

Cohn Consulting Group, who provided unwavering support for this effort.

I want to express my thanks to Ted Cohn, who first inspired me about consulting, and to Larry Zagarola, my mentor and my dear friend, for providing so much guidance and freedom in developing both as a person and as a professional and for his advice to always "take chances." This book was one of those chances.

A good consultant learns as much from clients as he imparts to them. There are so many clients who have helped me grow but five in particular I would like to thank specifically: Bob Karnell, Ross Born, David Schaffer, Mr. B., and Jordan Glatt. To each of you, my deepest gratitude for the lessons learned

Finally, thanks to my wife Barbara and my daughters Amy and Casie, from whom I have learned the greatest lesson, balance.

# About the Authors

**David F. Giannetto** is the director of Cohn Consulting Group's Enterprise Performance Management Practice, and has been with J.H. Cohn LLP since 1999. He is responsible for helping client organizations improve operations efficiency, management effectiveness, customer satisfaction, and systems integration through the implementation of the latest performance management methodologies. Prior to this, he was an operations manager and quality auditor for Airborne Express Freight Corporation (currently DHL) at locations throughout northern New Jersey and New York City.

David is a former U.S. logistics officer who served with the 10th Mountain Division and is a Distinguished Military Graduate of Rutgers University, earning a business management degree from Monmouth University. He is following in the footsteps of his father, Vincent Giannetto III, one of the nation's most collectable and respected decoy carvers, who has won awards as both a decoy carver and wildlife photographer. Originally taught piano by his aunt at age 10, he is a lifelong musician whose work has been published by two private record labels. Born and raised in Edgewater Park, New Jersey, he currently resides in Basking Ridge, New Jersey.

## About the Authors

**Anthony Zecca** is the partner-in-charge of Cohn Consulting Group, a division of J.H. Cohn LLP, one of the country's largest accounting and consulting firms.

Tony is an expert in driving corporate performance, developing business intelligence systems, and creating highly functional management teams. He has worked with top management to assess overall organizational effectiveness and strategic alignment, and to improve management effectiveness, profitability, and cash flow. Tony is an accomplished financial and management professional and a seasoned strategist focused on helping clients develop and implement growth and profit strategies that obtain breakthrough results within varying economic and market environments. He has served as the chief operating officer (COO) for several companies on the strategies and concepts consultants talk about, but rarely implement. In this capacity, he had overall management control and responsibility for the financial and operational areas, and was responsible for successfully driving both top- and bottom-line performance.

Tony earned a Bachelor of Science degree in accounting from Fairleigh Dickinson University, Teaneck, New Jersey. He has been very active in community activities and on various boards and business associations, including the American Institute of Certified Public Accountants (AICPA), and the National Association of Corporate Directors (NACD). Tony is a certified public accountant in New Jersey and New York.

# Index

# Index

# Index

# Index

# Index